THE TABERNACLE:
SHADOWS
OF THE MESSIAH
ITS SACRIFICES, SERVICES, AND PRIESTHOOD

by David M. Levy

The Friends of Israel Gospel Ministry, Inc.
P. O. Box 908, Bellmawr, NJ 08099

THE TABERNACLE: Shadows of the Messiah

David M. Levy

Copyright © 1993 by The Friends of Israel Gospel Ministry, Inc.
Bellmawr, NJ 08099

Eighth Printing 2003

Library of Congress Catalog Card Number: 93-71931
ISBN 0-915540-17-7

Cover and inside illustrations by Stan Stein, Stein Studios, Northfield, NJ

Visit our Web site at www.foi.org.

PREFACE

N umerous books have been written on the Old Testament
Tabernacle, but few new works on the subject have
appeared in recent years. Those published make little or no
mention of the priesthood that served in the Tabernacle, and
even less is said about the sacrifices offered there. New books on
the Tabernacle are often sketchy in their presentation, overly
fanciful in their typology, or provide exaggerated anti-types of
Christ that were never intended by the writers of Scripture.

Unfortunately, there is scant preaching or teaching about the
Tabernacle in most churches today. The subject is often relegat-
ed to a few lessons in Sunday school or given a quick gloss over
while studying the Book of Exodus. But the opposite is true in
the Bible. Few people realize the great importance given to the
Tabernacle throughout Scripture. Only two chapters of the Bible
are devoted to a description of the creation of the world and
mankind, but 50 chapters are devoted to a description of the
Tabernacle and its related ministries.

Believers should study the Tabernacle and its ministries for
the following reasons:

1. Study of the Tabernacle is necessary for a proper
   understanding of God's redemptive program, which is
   progressively revealed throughout Scripture.
2. An understanding of the Tabernacle informs sinful people
   about the holiness of God.
3. Knowledge of the Tabernacle is foundational to an understanding of Christ's fulfillment of God's redemptive program.

4. The Tabernacle demonstrates how a holy God can rightfully manifest His grace and mercy to sinful people.

5. The priestly ministry in the Tabernacle reveals how sinful people can approach a holy God with acceptable worship.

6. Study of the priesthood is foundational to an understanding of Christ's priestly ministry.

7. Understanding the function of Israel's priesthood enables Christians to have a greater appreciation of their own role as believer-priests.

8. The sacrificial system within the Tabernacle teaches the great importance God placed on the need for a blood sacrifice to atone for sin.

9. A proper understanding of the Levitical sacrifices gives Christians a greater understanding of God's view of the various degrees of sin in the Old Testament.

10. A good grasp of the Tabernacle is necessary to understand more than half of the Book of Hebrews, as well as other portions of the New Testament.

Those who study the Tabernacle often find it extremely difficult to put their research into a systematic format that adequately conveys its true meaning and typology as fulfilled by Christ. For this reason, the author has tried to approach the subject simply, systematically, and scripturally. He has not endeavored to pen a profound work on the Tabernacle but, rather, to write in such a way that both those with little Bible knowledge and those with many years of personal Bible study will be inspired and blessed by reading about this very important subject. Unlike most books on the subject, the author has structured his material in a way that will save many hours of personal study for laymen, teachers, and ministers who desire a comprehensive view of the Tabernacle.

Contents

PART I
THE TABERNACLE

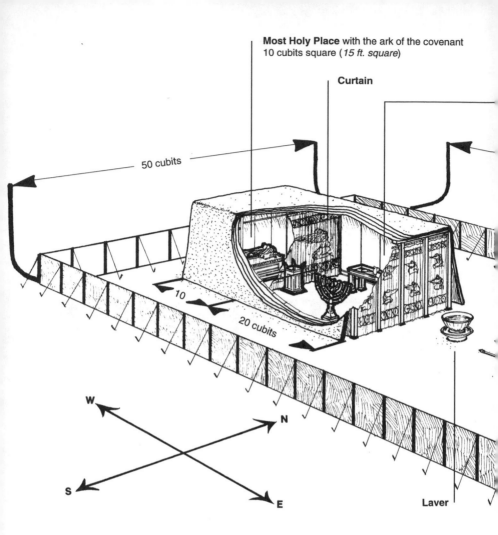

Most Holy Place with the ark of the covenant
10 cubits square (*15 ft. square*)

Curtain

50 cubits

10

20 cubits

W

N

S

E

Laver

Layout of the Tabernacle

Holy Place, with the golden table for the bread of the Presence, golden lampstand, and altar of incense.
    length: 20 cubits (30 ft.)
    width:: 10 cubits (15 ft.)

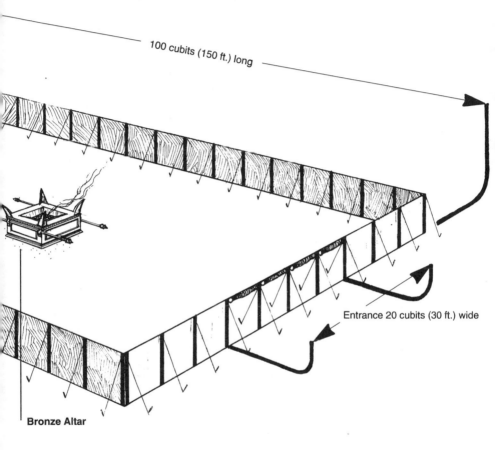

100 cubits (150 ft.) long

Entrance 20 cubits (30 ft.) wide

Bronze Altar

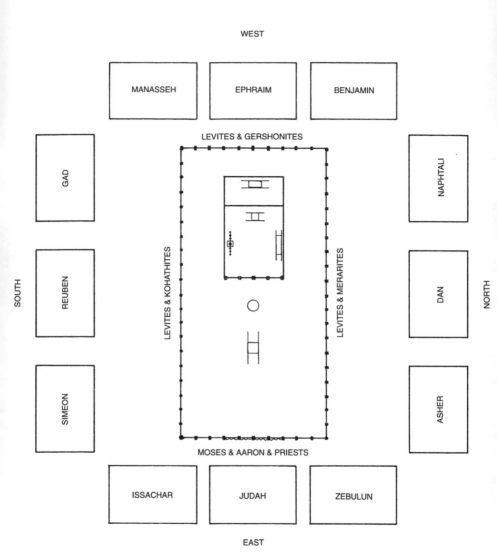

WEST

MANASSEH   EPHRAIM   BENJAMIN

LEVITES & GERSHONITES

GAD

NAPHTALI

SOUTH

REUBEN

LEVITES & KOHATHITES

LEVITES & MERARITES

DAN

NORTH

SIMEON

ASHER

MOSES & AARON & PRIESTS

ISSACHAR   JUDAH   ZEBULUN

EAST

The Encampment

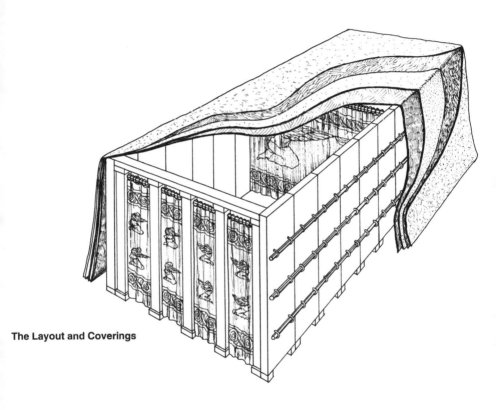

The Layout and Coverings

And the LORD *spoke unto Moses, saying, Speak unto the children of Israel, that they bring me an offering: of every man that giveth it willingly with his heart ye shall take my offering . . . And let them make me a sanctuary, that I may dwell among them. According to all that I show thee, after the pattern of the tabernacle, and the pattern of all the furnishings thereof, even so shall ye make it.*

Exodus 25:1–2, 8–9

CHAPTER 1

The Tabernacle
(Exodus 25:1–9)

" **I** have been to the mountain, and I have seen the glory of the Lord," would be the testimony of Moses if he were here today. Think how Moses must have felt when he heard the piercing sound as God thundered from Mount Sinai, "Come up to me" (Ex. 24:12). How he must have sensed the drawing power of God when he left Aaron, Hur, Joshua, and the elders of Israel to ascend into the presence of God. What awe must have filled his being when, at the summit, he experienced the envelopment of God's glory.

For six days, Moses sat in silent contemplation waiting for direction from God. Then, suddenly, the silence was broken on the seventh day when God spoke to Moses out of the cloud, "Speak unto the children of Israel . . . And let them make me a sanctuary, that I may dwell among them. According to all that I show thee, after the pattern of the tabernacle, and the pattern of all the furnishings thereof, even so shall ye make it" (Ex. 25:2, 8–9).

The God of Israel—who had redeemed them from the bondage of Egypt, revealed His glory to them on Mount Sinai, and given them His law to live by—now condescended to dwell in their midst. What joy must have swept over Moses when he saw the plans for the Tabernacle that he was to build and heard that the God of the universe would dwell among the Israelites.

The Tabernacle is of such great importance to God's redemptive program that 50 chapters in the Bible are given to explaining its pattern, construction, and service. Nothing was left to Moses' speculation; God revealed to him in minute detail every aspect of the Tabernacle. More than 20 times in Exodus we read, "as the Lord commanded Moses."

Five names in Scripture describe the Tabernacle. It was called "a sanctuary" (Ex. 25:8), denoting that it was set apart for a holy God. "Tabernacle" (Ex. 25:9) reveals that it was the dwelling place of God among His people. "Tent" (Ex. 26:36) designated it as a temporary dwelling place of God. It was called "the tabernacle of the congregation" (Ex. 29:42) because it was where God met with His people. The final expression, "the tabernacle of testimony" (Ex. 38:21), described the law given to Moses, which was kept in the ark of the covenant located in the holy of holies. What an appropriate appellation for the Tabernacle, which stood as a testimony to Israel and the world of God's truth and glory.

The Purpose of the Tabernacle

For almost 500 years, the Tabernacle served as a place for God to dwell among His people and a place where His people could commune with Him (Ex. 25:8; 40:34–37). Throughout Israel's history, there was a propensity toward idolatry; thus, the Tabernacle stood as a visual reminder to Israel that they served the true and living God. It helped keep Israel from the idol worship that was practiced by those living around them as they made their pilgrimage in the wilderness.

Although the Tabernacle made God accessible to the Israelites, He was only approachable in holiness. The structure and service of the Tabernacle showed a sinful people how they could come before a holy God in worship and service (Ex. 29:42–43, 45), offer sacrifice for sin (Lev. 1—7; 16—17), and receive instruction and counsel from the Word of God. Thus, it was a graphic portrayal of God's redemptive program for Israel. Every aspect of the Tabernacle—from the brazen altar, where sacrifices were offered for sin, to the mediating high priest, who offered the sacrificial blood on the mercy seat—pointed to God's redemptive plan. The people could only approach God through a blood atonement and a mediating priesthood.

This fact is beautifully typified in the ministry of Jesus the Messiah, who left His throne in heaven and tabernacled among His people (Jn. 1:14). In Christ we have a high priest, a perfect blood sacrifice, and access to God for all who put their trust in Him.

The Pattern of the Tabernacle

The Tabernacle was an ingenious, prefabricated structure that could be moved at will. Its construction was a cooperative task between God and the people. The Lord provided the pattern of the Tabernacle (Ex. 25:9); the people provided the materials (Ex. 25:3–7) by bringing an offering with willing hearts (Ex. 25:2). The offerings they brought were gold, silver, brass, jewels, fine linens, and dye from Egypt; goat hair and ram skins from their flocks; seal skins (porpoises) from the Red Sea; and shittim (acacia) wood from the Sinai. Moses was instructed to take the offerings only if they came from willing hearts. Today, God desires that His people give themselves to His service first (Rom. 12:1) and then bring their gifts, "not grudgingly, or of necessity" (2 Cor. 9:7) but willingly, for His work. God's plan has always been to accomplish His purposes through redeemed people.

The Tabernacle was the focal point of Israel's community and life, with the tribes dwelling around its four sides (Num. 2). On the east side were 186,000 people from the tribes of Issachar, Judah, and Zebulun; on the north side were 157,000 people from the tribes of Asher, Dan, and Naphtali; on the west side were 108,100 people from the tribes of Manasseh, Ephraim, and

Benjamin; and on the south side were 151,400 people from the tribes of Simeon, Reuben, and Gad. This did not include Moses, Aaron, the Priests, and the Levites (Kohathites, Gershonites, and Merarites), who numbered approximately 22,300 and were placed on all four sides of the Tabernacle. The number of men 20 years of age and older (not including the Levites) was 603,550 (Num. 1:45–46). Including the women, children, and the remainder of the mixed multitude who left Egypt, the number of people encamped around the Tabernacle was probably between 2,500,000 and 3,000,000. Adding the animals the Israelites brought with them from Egypt made this a huge encampment, to say the least. One author estimated that the encampment around the Tabernacle extended approximately 12 square miles. Another author has estimated that the provisions needed to meet the needs of the people and animals were in excess of 30 boxcars of food and 300 tank cars of water per day. If the people traveled 50 abreast, the procession would have stretched for 40 miles.

The outer court was 150 feet long and 75 feet wide, enclosed by a fine-twined linen curtain seven and a half feet high. Its gate, which was placed on the east side of the court, was 30 feet wide.

The fine-twined linen curtain was held in place by 60 pillars made of acacia wood and covered with bronze; they were spaced seven and a half feet apart. Each pillar was secured in a bronze socket with cords fastened at the top and tied to the ground with a bronze stake. The pillars were made more secure by a silver bar that connected them near the top, from which the linen curtains were hung. Each pillar was crowned with a silver capital.

When entering the court, people were overwhelmed at the beautiful furnishings of gold and brass, which were dazzling to the eye.

The furniture and its placement—from the brazen altar to the mercy seat—typified the various ministries of Christ on our behalf. The Tabernacle with its ordinances was only "a figure for the time then present" (Heb. 9:9) but looked toward Christ's sacrificial death, which was to mediate a new covenant by means of His shed blood for the redemption of mankind (Heb. 9:11–22). The earthly Tabernacle was only a figure of the true Tabernacle in heaven, where Christ is enthroned in His high priestly ministry (Heb. 9:23–24).

The brazen altar stood in the outer court just inside the gate facing the Tabernacle (Ex. 40:6). The sacrificial animals were offered on this altar, and their blood was shed for the sins of the people. The brazen altar typifies Christ's redemptive work on the cross on our behalf, whereby all who put their faith in His shed blood are justified and receive remission of sins (Rom. 3:24–25). Just as it was impossible for the Israelites to come into God's presence without sacrificing at the brazen altar, so it is impossible today for people to come into the presence of God except by the ministry of the cross.

The brazen laver stood in the outer court between the brazen altar and the Tabernacle. The laver was provided only for the priests, who had to wash before entering the Tabernacle. As they washed in the laver, mirrors reflected their images, reminding them of how God saw them. The laver speaks of Christ as our sanctification. As believer-priests, we are reminded that Christ has sanctified us for His service and is sanctifying us by cleansing us from the daily defilement of sin "with the washing of water by the word" (Eph. 5:26).

From the laver, the priest walked a few paces to the Tabernacle, drew back the curtain, and entered into the holy place, where he could have fellowship with God.

The Tabernacle proper was 15 feet wide, 45 feet long, and 15 feet high. It was divided into two sections, the holy place (15 feet wide and 30 feet long) and the holy of holies (15 feet square). Forty-eight boards comprised the walls, 20 each on the north and south sides, six on the west side, and two corner boards. Each board was 15 feet long and 27 inches wide, covered with gold, and set on two golden tenors, which were secured in silver bases. The boards were held together by five golden rods, four on the outside and one on the inside.

The whole structure had four coverings: first, an inner lining of embroidered, fine-twined linen; second, a woven goat hair covering over the linen; third, a ram skin covering, dyed red, over the goat hair; and fourth, a waterproof porpoise skin covering placed on the top. Most likely the ceiling was flat, although some scholars believe it may have made a peak, like a present-day tent. The holy place was entered through a hanging called the "door," and the holy of holies was entered through a veil (both will be described in later chapters).

There were three pieces of furniture in the holy place, and they typify our fellowship with Christ. The table of showbread stood on the right side in the holy place. The 12 loaves of bread on the table were a meal offering, representing the 12 tribes of Israel. The showbread typified Christ, who came down from heaven, and all who partake of Him have eternal life (Jn. 6:51). As the bread of life, Christ sustains the believer-priests who feed on Him.

On the left side of the holy place stood the seven-branched golden lampstand, which spoke of Christ as the light of the world (Jn. 9:5). All who trust in Him are given the light of life (Jn. 8:12). We are to hold forth the light of God's Word in this darkened world (Phil. 2:15-16) so that men can see our good works and glorify the Father (Mt. 5:14–16). The glory of God will light up the new Jerusalem, which will be our dwelling place throughout eternity (Rev. 21:23).

The altar of incense stood in the holy place right in front of the veiled holy of holies. Burning coals from the brazen altar were placed on the altar of incense, over which sweet incense was poured daily. The smoke from the incense curled upward, representing the prayers of God's people (Ps. 141:1; Rev. 5:8). The altar typified Christ our high priest, who intercedes for us before the Father's throne (Jn. 17; Heb. 7:25), and the believer-priests, who offer up "the sacrifice of praise to God" (Heb. 13:15). The heavy veil that hung between the holy place and the holy of holies separated a holy God from a sinful people. Christ represents the veil, separating people from God. At His death on the cross, the veil was rent from top to bottom (Mt. 27:51), opening the way to God through His shed blood (Heb. 10:19) so that we can "come boldly unto the throne of grace, that we may obtain mercy" (Heb. 4:16).

Inside the holy of holies sat the ark of the covenant, a rectangular box covered with gold inside and out. On top of the ark stood two cherubim of God, facing each other but looking down toward the mercy seat, with their wings stretched out over it. It was on the mercy seat that the high priest sprinkled blood on the day of atonement, which enabled God to cover the sins of the high priest and the people. The people waited patiently outside the Tabernacle, their eyes fixed on it, wondering whether the high priest would reappear. If he reappeared, God had accepted the blood atonement, and their sins were covered for another year. Christ, as the believers' high priest (Heb. 7:24–25), offered His own blood to put away sin. He is the believers' propitiation (Rom. 3:25; 1 Jn. 2:2), satisfying the righteous demands of a holy God for the judgment of sin and opening the way for Him to freely forgive people of their sin.

How beautiful it is to see the shadowy patterns of the Tabernacle fulfilled in Jesus the Messiah, who has justified us by His blood, cleanses and feeds us through His Word, lights the path before us, and intercedes for us along the way. Because of Him we have access through the veil to the throne of grace, that we may obtain mercy on the merit of His blood, which has put away our sin.

The Church Prefigured in the Tabernacle

The Tabernacle prefigured the church. Paul stated that the church is "an holy temple in the Lord . . . for an habitation of God through the Spirit" (Eph. 2:21–22). The word *temple* is not the Temple with all its porches and surrounding buildings but the inner sanctuary—the holy of holies. Today God does not dwell in a physical structure but in a spiritual body called the church. The figure is very impressive. The Temple was holy and set apart for God's service; likewise, the church is holy and consecrated to

His service. Collectively, God dwells in each believer by the Holy Spirit, forming us into His Temple. The nation of Israel never experienced this privilege. Only the high priest was able to enter into the holy of holies and stand in the presence of God, and that only once a year. This privilege should cause each believer in the church to walk circumspectly before the Lord.

The Tabernacle also prefigures individual Christians. Paul said, "Know ye not that your body is the temple [sanctuary] of the Holy Spirit who is in you, whom ye have of God, and ye are not your own?" (1 Cor. 6:19). As a sanctuary where the Spirit of God dwells, believers are not at liberty to allow their bodies to be used outside of His designed purposes for them.

The Tabernacle, with its many symbols and types, was a shadow pointing to the Savior who, in the fullness of God's time, tabernacled in this world and opened the way for God to bring redemption to mankind. The writer of the Book of Hebrews aptly summed up Christ's ministry when he stated, "But Christ being come an high priest of good things to come, by a greater and more perfect tabernacle, not made with hands, that is to say, not of this building, Neither by the blood of goats and calves, but by his own blood he entered in once into the holy place, having obtained eternal redemption for us" (Heb. 9:11–12).

As we look at the ministry of the Tabernacle fulfilled in Christ, may the words "I have been to the mountain, and I have seen the glory of the Lord" be your testimony through this study, as the shadows of the Tabernacle set forth the reality of the Savior.

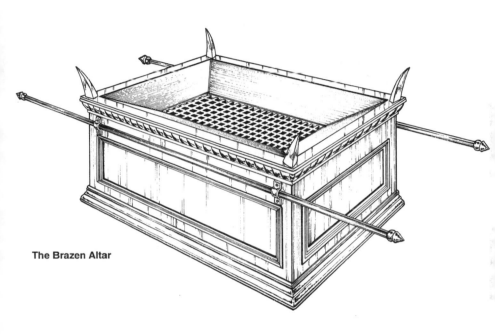

The Brazen Altar

23

And thou shalt make an altar of acacia wood, five cubits long, and five cubits broad: the altar shall be foursquare; and the height thereof shall be three cubits. And thou shalt make the horns of it upon the four corners thereof: its horns shall be of the same; and thou shalt overlay it with bronze. And thou shalt make its pans to receive its ashes, and its shovels, and its basins, and its fleshhooks, and its firepans: all the vessels thereof thou shalt make of bronze. And thou shalt make for it a grate of network of bronze; and upon the net shalt thou make four bronze rings in the four corners thereof.

Exodus 27:1–4

C H A P T E R   2

The Brazen Altar
(Exodus 27:1–8)

The Tabernacle stood in all its glory with the 12 tribes camped around it. How inspiring it must have seemed to the Israelites as they gazed upon its colorful gates and beautifully sculptured furnishings of gold, silver, and brass glistening in the sunlight. From their tents they could see the visible presence of God's glory hovering over it in the form of a cloud by day and a pillar of fire by night, assuring them of His guiding presence. Come, let us enter the court and witness what was involved in the ministry at the brazen altar.

The Structure of the Altar and Its Significance

Slowly the Israelites reverently approached the Tabernacle, drew back the curtain, and entered its court to present their sacrifices. Upon entering the court, they stood in awe, gazing at the blood-stained altar, as the smoke from previous sacrifices curled into the sky. The altar was a very simple hollow box made of shittim (acacia) wood, overlaid with brass, seven and a half feet square, stood four

and a half feet high, and had four horns pointing outward at each corner (vv. 1–2). A brass grate extended through its middle in which
brass rings were fastened at each corner; wooden staves covered with
brass were put through the rings for carrying the altar. The altar was
not Moses' creation; God had revealed it to him on the mount. It
stood just inside the court gate (Ex. 40:6), facing the Tabernacle. It was
the largest piece of furniture used in worship and was always open
to guilty Israelites so they could atone for their sin.

For Christians, the altar is full of symbolic meaning and spiritual teaching. Shittim (acacia) wood is a hard, incorruptible,
indestructible wood that grows in the Sinai Desert. It beautifully
portrays the humanity of Christ, who came from "a root out of a
dry ground" (Isa. 53:2) and was sinless in His human nature
(Heb. 4:15; 7:26). The indestructibility of the wood speaks of
Christ in His humanity, which withstood the fire of crucifixion
(Jn. 10:18) and the decaying effect of the grave (Acts 2:31), and
His body, which was victoriously resurrected (Mt. 28:5–6).

The brass covering over the shittim wood typified the divine
righteousness and judgment of Christ, the righteous one (1 Jn.
3:5), who took the divine judgment of God upon Himself and
bore our judgment on the cross by becoming sin for us (2 Cor.
5:21). As the Israelites were saved from death when they looked
at the brass serpent that Moses held up in the wilderness, so all
who trust in Jesus Christ, who was lifted up on the cross as a sacrifice for sin, will be saved from damnation (Jn. 3:14–15). Christ's
appearance to John on the Isle of Patmos with "feet like fine
bronze, as if they burned in a furnace" (Rev. 1:15) spoke of His
judicial character in judging His enemies at the Second Coming.

The four horns on the corners of the altar spoke of power (cp.
1 Sam. 2:1–10; 2 Sam. 22:3) and were used in binding the sacrifice
to the altar (Ps. 118:27). They were also sprinkled with the blood
of the sacrifice (Ex. 29:12). The sacrifice tied to the horns pointed
to Christ's unfaltering commitment to carry out the Father's will
(Heb. 10:5–7) when He allowed Himself to be nailed to the cross
as our blood atonement (Mt. 26:39, 42). His shed blood on the
cross expiates the sins of all those who are willing to put their

faith in His sacrificial death (Rom. 3:25–26). The blood-stained horns pointed upward and outward to the four corners of the world, reminding us of the saving power of Christ's blood that will be witnessed throughout the world (Acts 1:8).

The Sacrifice at the Altar and Its Significance

The brazen altar was provided for sacrifice. Without sacrifice, there could be no atonement for sin (Lev. 17:11; Heb. 9:22). Soberly, the Israelites brought the prescribed offerings without spot or blemish to the priests, who stood at the Tabernacle's gate to receive them. The offerers laid their hands on the heads of the offerings, symbolic of their identification with their substitutionary death on their behalf—their sins were transferred to the sacrifices, and the life of the sacrifices was transferred to them. The offerers then killed the animals, while the priests caught the sacrificial blood in a basin to be offered as an atonement. The priests, functioning as mediators, sprinkled the blood of the sacrifices on the altar and poured the remaining blood in the basin at the altar's base. Then the priests cut the sacrifices into pieces, washed the inner parts, and burned various pieces on the altar as a sweet savor to the Lord.

At the altar, an innocent lamb bore the judgment of the guilty. Christ, the believers' lamb (Jn. 1:29; Rev. 13:8), died on the altar of the cross to bear the judgment of God's wrath against sin on our behalf (Isa. 53:3–6; Rom. 4:25). The sacrifice being burnt on the altar as a sweet savor to God (Lev. 1:9) typified Christ, who was offered up as "a sacrifice to God for a sweet-smelling savor" (Eph. 5:2).

The word *altar* means *high place*. The sacrifice had to be lifted up on the elevated altar (Lev. 9:22). Christ's being lifted up on the cross as our sacrifice speaks of this procedure: "And, as Moses lifted up the serpent in the wilderness, even so must the Son of man be lifted up" (Jn. 3:14).

The fire that burned continually on the altar had a twofold meaning. It proclaimed God's holiness and justice, and it was symbolic of His readiness to receive the sacrificial offerings of the people to cleanse them from sin.

The Serving Utensils at the Altar and Their Significance

The five utensils used to serve the altar were types of Christ. Pans and shovels were used to remove the precious ashes of the sacrifices and carry them outside the camp to be disposed of in a clean place. The ashes spoke of the finished work of Christ (Jn. 19:30), who was put into a clean place (a new sepulcher) at His burial (Jn. 19:41). The blood from the sacrifices was drained into a basin and poured out at the base of the altar, typifying Christ, who poured out His blood on our behalf (Heb. 9:12–15). The flesh hooks represented the cruel hands of the men who nailed Christ to the cross (Lk. 23:33). The fire pans (censers), which carried the fire from the brazen altar to the altar of incense, represented Christ's intercessory ministry of prayer at the Father's throne (Heb. 7:25) as our advocate (1 Jn. 2:1).

The Salvation That the Altar Symbolized

The brazen altar and the cross of Christ both speak of justification. Justification does not mean *made* righteous but *declared* righteous—put into a right relationship with God (Rom. 4:24–25). Thus, justification is a judicial act of God whereby He declares us righteous when we trust in Jesus Christ's work on the cross on our behalf. In the days of the Tabernacle, the Israelites were restored to a right relationship with God by offering a blood atonement on the altar; today, Jews and Gentiles are restored by appropriating the atoning blood of Christ to take away sins. Justification is not obtained by any work that we do but is bestowed freely through the grace of God (Rom. 4:24), resulting in the removal of the guilt and punishment of sin, the righteousness of Christ being imputed to our lives, and our restoration to favor and fellowship with God (Rom. 4:25).

The position of the altar spoke of access and fellowship with God. It stood inside the court facing the door of the Tabernacle. Before the priest could pass to the Tabernacle, he had to offer a blood sacrifice on the brazen altar. Today, access and fellowship with God can come only through the sacrificial death of Christ (1 Tim. 2:5; Heb. 9:15).

Approaching the Tabernacle of God without offering a proper sacrifice on the altar meant certain death. If we reject the meritorious sacrifice of Christ's work on the cross, we will be separated from God and face eternal death (Jn. 3:36; 1 Jn. 5:12).

God requires another sacrifice from believers. They are to present themselves as "a living sacrifice" to God (Rom. 12:1). The words of Paul ably sum up our consecration: "I am crucified with Christ: nevertheless I live; yet not I, but Christ liveth in me; and the life which I now live in the flesh I live by the faith of the Son of God, who loved me and gave himself for me" (Gal. 2:20).

Have you committed your life as "a living sacrifice" to God? Unless you allow Christ to control the altar of your life, you will not be able to manifest a fruitful walk in service for Him. Why not draw back the curtain of your life and offer it on the altar of sacrifice for God's service? As believer-priests, we must be continually cleansed from sin before we can enter into God's service. As we continue reading, we will approach the brazen laver and see what is involved in our cleansing for spiritual service.

The Brazen Laver

And the Lord spoke unto Moses, saying, Thou shalt also make a laver of bronze, and its foot also of bronze, with which to wash. And thou shalt put it between the tabernacle of the congregation and the altar, and thou shalt put water therein; For Aaron and his sons shall wash their hands and their feet thereat. When they go into the tabernacle of the congregation, they shall wash with water, that they die not; or when they come near to the altar to minister, to burn offering made by fire unto the Lord.

Exodus 30:17–20

CHAPTER 3

The Brazen Laver
(Exodus 30:17–21; 38:8; 40:7)

His hands splattered with blood and his feet soiled from the dust of the Tabernacle court, the priest moved quickly but reverently to the brazen laver for cleansing. The words of Moses were fresh in his mind each time he was called on to serve: "they shall wash with water, that they die not" (Ex. 30:20). Purification before and during service in the Tabernacle was mandatory for the priests who ministered before God.

The laver was never used by the congregation but was provided exclusively for the priests' purification. During their consecration to the priesthood, they had been washed thoroughly at the laver according to the command of Moses: "And Aaron and his sons thou shalt bring unto the door of the tabernacle of the congregation, and shalt wash them with water" (Ex. 29:4).

Each year the high priest washed on the day of atonement, put on the holy linen garments, and made an atonement for himself and the children of Israel (Lev. 16:24). But on every other day of the year, the priests only had to wash the defilement from their hands and feet before entering the Tabernacle to serve.

Carefully dipping their right hands into the laver, they meticulously washed their right hands then their right feet; reversing
the process, they washed their left hands and left feet.

The Strategic Position of the Laver

The priests knew all too well the strategic placement and
symbolic meaning of the laver. Their sins being atoned for at
the brazen altar made it possible for them to approach the
Tabernacle in worship, but not before they stopped at the
brazen laver to wash the defilement of the dusty Tabernacle
court from their bodies. They had to be both spiritually and
physically clean before they could enter into the presence of
a holy God in communion and fellowship. The Word of God
was clear on this matter: "ye shall be holy; for I am holy"
(Lev. 11:44).

The brazen laver stood in the outer court between the brazen
altar and the Tabernacle. It had two parts: the circular brass bowl
made from the polished brass mirrors that the women brought
with them from Egypt, and the brass foot or pedestal (Ex. 38:8).
Although the size of the laver is not given, it had to be big
enough to hold the large amount of water used exclusively by
the priests for purification. Fresh spring water, probably from a
smitten rock, was poured continually into the laver for daily
purification. The laver had no measurements, symbolic of the
limitless cleansing power of God.

The Sanctifying Provision of the Laver

The laver was used only by the priests for purification. We
who have put our faith in Jesus Christ are called believer-priests.
We are also called "a chosen generation, a royal priesthood, an
holy nation, a people of his own" (1 Pet. 2:9); therefore, we can
offer spiritual sacrifices and praise that are "acceptable to God
by Jesus Christ" (1 Pet. 2:5; cp. 1 Pet. 2:9). As Aaron and his sons
were born into the priesthood (Ex. 28:1), so each of us enters the
priesthood by means of the new birth through the "washing [i.e.,
bath] of regeneration" (Ti. 3:5) in the blood of Jesus Christ. We

who have been washed from our sins in the blood of Jesus have been made a "kingdom of priests" (Rev. 1:5–6).

The ministry of the laver is of great spiritual significance in our Christian experience. In the brazen altar we see our justification. In the brazen laver we see our sanctification. The water in the laver typified our cleansing through the Word of God. When Jesus left the upper room and headed toward the Garden of Gethsemane just before His betrayal, He stopped in the vineyard of the Kidron Valley and gave the parable of the vine and branches. He said every branch that bears fruit must be purged so that it might bring forth more fruit. Then He told His disciples, "Now ye are clean through the word which I have spoken unto you" (Jn. 15:3). The Holy Spirit sanctifies and cleanses us, preparing us for service in Christ.

The word *sanctified* means to be *set apart*. First, we are set apart from sin, both spiritually (2 Chr. 29:5, 15–18) and physically (1 Th. 4:3). Second, we are set apart for divine service through Christ our high priest (1 Cor. 1:2; 6:11).

Sanctification is described in three ways. First, we are *positionally sanctified*. We are eternally sanctified to God the moment we accept the atoning work of Jesus Christ for our justification (Heb. 10:10, 14; 13:12). Instantaneously we are separated from sin unto salvation. It is called positional sanctification because it signifies a position or standing before God that does not depend on our daily walk for its maintenance, although this position should lead us to holy living.

Second, we are *progressively being sanctified*, a process whereby we are daily sanctified as we walk in obedience before God, separating ourselves from sin and allowing the Holy Spirit to cleanse us through the truth of the Word of God (Jn. 17:17). Believers progress in sanctification as they appropriate and apply the Word of God to their lives (2 Tim. 2:19–21; 2 Pet. 3:18).

Third, we will be *perfected in sanctification*. Believers are promised an ultimate (complete) sanctification. We will be perfected when we receive our resurrected bodies at the Second Coming of the Lord (Eph. 5:27). At that time, we will be conformed to the image of Jesus Christ (Rom. 8:29), for we shall be like Him (1 Jn. 3:2).

Four agents are involved in our sanctification. The Father chastens us for sin (Heb. 12:10); the Son provides the means for our sanctification through His shed blood (Heb. 13:12); the Holy Spirit applies the truth of God's Word to our lives (2 Th. 2:13; 1 Pet. 1:2); and we are to separate ourselves voluntarily from sin (2 Cor. 7:1).

The Servant's Purification by the Lord

The need for purification in our walk was beautifully illustrated during the final hours of our Lord's ministry on earth (Jn. 13:1–10). Rising from the Passover table, Jesus took a towel and a basin of water and began to wash the disciples' feet.

When it was Peter's turn to be washed, he blurted out, "Thou shalt never wash my feet" (v. 8). Jesus quickly informed Peter, "If I wash thee not, thou hast no part with me" (v. 8).

Jesus was not saying that if He did not wash Peter's feet, Peter could not have a relationship with Him, for his relationship with the Lord had already been established. Rather, Jesus was saying that if He did not wash Peter's feet, Peter could not have fellowship or communion with Him. As usual, the impetuous Peter went overboard and responded, "Lord, not my feet only, but also my hands and my head" (v. 9). Jesus answered, "He that is washed needeth not except to wash his feet" (v. 10). The words *washed* and *wash* in verse 10 have different meanings. The word *washed* (Gr., *louo*) means to *bathe one's body completely*. It speaks of the complete ablution that takes place when we are declared justified at the moment of salvation. The word *wash* (Gr., *nipto*) is used of those who wash their hands and feet, symbolizing sanctification. The picture is of people returning home from a public bathhouse. Their bodies being completely bathed, they need only wash the dust from their feet to be clean when they enter their houses.

By washing the disciples' feet, the Lord taught that we who have been thoroughly cleansed through His blood must still be cleansed in our daily walk with Him. Daily sins must be confessed to God in order to maintain an unbroken communion and fellowship with Him. John explicitly stated this when he wrote, "If we say that we have no sin, we deceive ourselves, and the truth is not in us. If we confess our sins, he is faithful and just to forgive us our sins, and to cleanse us from all unrighteousness" (1 Jn. 1:8–9).

When the priests washed at the laver, they saw their images reflected from the brass mirrors used in its construction. We have already seen that brass typified Christ in His ministry of judgment. The mirrors spoke of the Word of God, which reveals and reflects our sinful purposes and intentions. The writer of the Book of Hebrews put it well when he wrote, "For the word of God is living, and powerful, and sharper than any two-edged sword, piercing even to the dividing asunder of soul and spirit, and of the joints and marrow, and is a discerner of the thoughts and intents of the heart" (Heb. 4:12). On the day of judgment, Christ will judge people on the basis of the Word of God (Jn. 12:48).

The brass also speaks of the believers' self-judgment, which they are expected to exercise when they sin. Paul said, "For if we would judge ourselves, we should not be judged" (1 Cor. 11:31). If we refuse to judge our own sins, the Lord will chasten us (Heb. 12:6) back to communion and fellowship, so that we will "not be condemned with the world" (1 Cor. 11:32). The chastening process is not enjoyable; in fact, it can be very grievous, but it produces righteousness and holiness (Heb. 12:10–11). If Christians persist in their sins after being chastened by the Lord, He may bring judgment on them in the form of weakness, sickness, or even premature death (1 Cor. 11:30). The Word of God, appropriated and properly applied, prevents us from falling into sin, keeps us in our walk before the Lord, and makes our fellowship sweet in Him.

The Servant's Privilege Before the Lord

As believer-priests who have been justified and sanctified, we are now ready to offer worship and service to the Lord. The greatest privilege of all is to have direct access into the presence of God (Heb. 10:19–22)—something the Old Testament believers did not have. The priests, being cleansed for service, were prepared to enter the holy place for communion with a holy God.

We who are cleansed in our walk before God are prepared to do the same thing.

David summed up the believers' standing before the Lord very clearly when he wrote, "Who shall ascend into the hill of the LORD? Or who shall stand in his holy place? He who hath clean hands, and a pure heart" (Ps. 24:3–4). We who have been cleansed by the washing of the water by the Word of God will receive, as the psalmist said, "blessing from the LORD, and righteousness from the God of his salvation" (Ps. 24:5).

We must respond to the Lord's admonishment, "But, as he who hath called you is holy, so be ye holy in all manner of life, Because it is written, Be ye holy; for I am holy" (1 Pet. 1:15–16). Only then will we be able to walk through the veil into the holy presence of our Lord and then forward into each new day prepared for spiritual service for Him.

The Golden Lampstand

And thou shalt make a lampstand of pure gold: of beaten work shall the lampstand be made; its shaft, and its branches, its bowls, its knobs, and its flowers, shall be of the same.

Exodus 25:31

C H A P T E R   4

The Golden Lampstand

(Exodus 25:31–40; 37:17–24; 39:37)

aving been cleansed by washing at the brazen laver, the priest reverently made his way a few feet toward the Tabernacle entrance. His heart pounded with anticipation as he carefully drew back the heavy curtain of the Tabernacle and entered to minister in the holy place. A hush fell over him as he contemplated the privilege and responsibility of representing his people before a holy God. In a spirit of humility, he worshiped and communed with the true and living God.

The Tabernacle was a rectangular building divided into two sections. The holy place was 30 feet long and 15 feet wide, and the holy of holies was 15 feet square. The holy place and the holy of holies were divided by a huge, heavy veil made of blue, purple, scarlet, and fine-twined linen, richly embroidered with figures of cherubim (Ex. 26:31–33). Three pieces of furniture graced the holy place. The golden lampstand stood on the left side (south); the table of showbread stood on the right side (north); and the altar of incense stood in front of the veiled entrance to the holy of holies, which contained the ark of the

covenant. The furnishings were made from the exact specifica-
tions that God gave to Moses on Mount Sinai (Ex. 25:40).

Light from the huge golden lampstand filled every corner of
the holy place with a warm, shimmering brilliance, providing
illumination for the priest as he ministered. The lampstand was
made of one talent of pure gold (Ex. 25:39), which weighed 90
pounds. With gold selling at approximately $350 an ounce, the
cost to reproduce it today would be tremendous. The lampstand
had a center stem with three branches on each side, making it a
seven-pronged lampstand. Each stem had three groups of
almond blossom cups, knobs, and flowers—except the middle
stem, which had four (Ex. 25:31–40). It was not made from a
mold but was hammered out of a single talent of gold (Ex. 37:17,
24). The artisan who crafted it was given great ability by God to
be able to sculpt such a beautiful piece.

It was part of the priests' ministry to care for the lampstand.
Its lamps were kept perpetually burning (Ex. 27:20–21) by filling
them daily with pure olive oil. The priests trimmed each lamp
every evening and morning (Ex. 30:7–8) with pure gold tongs
and snuff dishes (Ex. 25:38).

The Lampstand and Christ

The lampstand was filled with rich symbolic teaching for
Christians. The gold in the lampstand typified the deity of
Christ, the divine Son of God, who stepped across the galaxies of
the universe and became a man. He was pure in His humanity,
having neither spot nor blemish (1 Pet. 1:19), but it was His deity
that sustained His humanity.

The lampstand, as we have already seen, was not molded or
pieced together but was hammered out of a solid talent of gold
(Ex. 25:31), symbolizing the Lord, who endured the harsh, hot
sting of a biting whip before His crucifixion (Mt. 27:26, 30). Isaiah
wrote concerning His suffering, "we did esteem him stricken,
smitten of God, and afflicted . . . and with his stripes we are
healed" (Isa. 53:4–5). Contemplate the stripes of the Lord, and
your love for Him will be renewed and deepened.

The dimensions of the lampstand are not given, but its size, weight, and beauty portray Christ in His fathomless greatness. He is the creator of all things, and by Him all things are held together (Col. 1:16–17). He is limitless in His value, for in Him are hidden all the treasures of wisdom and knowledge to be found (Col. 2:3). Paul summed up the greatness of Christ when he wrote, "For in him dwelleth all the fullness of the Godhead bodily" (Col. 2:9). Joy should fill our souls as we realize that we are complete in Him (Col. 2:10), the one who provides a wealth of wisdom and knowledge for our Christian walk.

The lampstand's purpose was to provide light. It was a beautiful type of Christ, who is the true light of the world. Jesus said, "I am the light of the world; he that followeth me shall not walk in darkness, but shall have the light of life" (Jn. 8:12). The "light of life" that Jesus spoke of can be obtained only through faith in His atoning work on the cross. But Jesus made it very clear that the world in general would not come to Him as the "light of life": "And this is the condemnation, that light is come into the world, and men loved darkness rather than light, because their deeds were evil" (Jn. 3:19).

The light in the holy place was symbolic of Christ's holiness. John wrote, "God is light, and in him is no darkness at all" (1 Jn. 1:5). The glory of our Lord will also illuminate the new Jerusalem in eternity: "And the city had no need of the sun, neither of the moon, to shine in it; for the glory of God did light it, and the Lamb is the lamp of it" (Rev. 21:23). Christians will enjoy the great privilege of walking in the glory of Christ's light throughout all eternity (Rev. 21:24).

The Lampstand and the Christian

The golden lampstand typified Christ, who lights up the walk and fellowship of believers. The holy place had no windows to allow light to shine into the Tabernacle. The light in the holy place was hidden from the world; only the priests had the privilege of ministering and enjoying the light of the lampstand. So it is with Christians. As believer-priests, we are able to enter into the light of fellowship and communion with God. John, who knew intimate fellowship with the Lord, wrote, "But if we walk in the light, as he is in the light, we have fellowship one with another" (1 Jn. 1:7).

Today, Christians are the only reflectors of Christ's light to a lost and dying world. Too often the light of believers shines dimly because it is hidden under a bushel (Mt. 5:15). Believers' lamps are to beam brightly, as a lighted city standing on a hill (Mt. 5:14) whose glow can be seen for miles around (Mt. 5:16).

The gold in the lampstand pictured the true faith that Christians possess. Jesus told the Laodicean church, "I counsel thee to buy of me gold tried in the fire, that thou mayest be rich" (Rev. 3:18). Christ, who is the pure gold, produces true faith in believers. Christians go through the hammering experience of suffering to try their faith so that it will come forth as gold tried in the fire. This type of faith is "much more precious than of gold that perisheth" (1 Pet. 1:7).

The golden lampstand was a type of the church. In Revelation chapters 2 and 3, the church is portrayed as a golden lampstand. Christ is the light of each lampstand and is to shine brightly through each of these local assemblies into the dark world of sin. Jesus warned the Ephesian church, who had lost its first love for Him, "repent, and do the first works, or else I will come unto thee quickly, and will remove thy lampstand out of its place" (Rev. 2:5). Sad to say, the light of all seven churches mentioned in Revelation 2 and 3 was removed, and today those churches do not exist. This situation should sound a solemn warning to the church of the 20th century to take heed, lest it suffer the same fate.

The Lampstand and the Comforter

The oil in the lampstand was a beautiful type of the ministry of the Holy Spirit. At the top of each branch were cups into which pure olive oil was poured. The oil produced the glowing light that filled the Tabernacle. The seven stems, olive oil, and flame are types of the Spirit's ministry, which was clearly taught by John: "And out of the throne proceeded lightnings and thunderclaps, and voices; and there were seven lamps of fire burning before the throne, which are the seven spirits of God" (Rev. 4:5). The "seven spirits of God"symbolize the perfection and fullness of the Spirit's ministry. The Holy Spirit is the person of the Godhead who administers the plans, purposes, and programs of God on earth.

First, the Holy Spirit played a major role in the Lord's life and ministry. He was conceived (Mt. 1:18–20), baptized (Mt. 3:16), anointed (Jn. 3:34; Heb. 1:9), empowered for service (Lk. 4:14, 18), and resurrected (Rom. 8:11) by the Holy Spirit.

In His opening words to the church at Sardis, the Lord said, "And unto the angel of the church in Sardis write: These things saith he that hath the seven spirits of God, and the seven stars" (Rev. 3:1). The "seven spirits of God" is a reference to the Holy Spirit in His sevenfold ministry, which Christ possesses.

Isaiah taught that the Holy Spirit will be manifested in a sevenfold ministry through Christ during the Kingdom age: "And there shall come forth a rod out of the stem of Jesse, and a Branch shall grow out of his roots; And the Spirit of the Lord shall rest upon him, the spirit of wisdom and understanding, the spirit of counsel and might, the spirit of knowledge and of the fear of the Lord" (Isa. 11:1–2).

It is interesting to parallel the sevenfold ministry of the Holy Spirit with the seven branches of the lampstand. In this context, the Holy Spirit is referred to as the "Spirit of the Lord" resting on Christ, who could be compared to the center shaft of the lampstand. Branching out of the stem were three branches on each side, corresponding to the ministry of the Holy Spirit of the Lord: the spirit of *wisdom* and *understanding*, the spirit of *counsel* and *might*, the spirit of *knowledge* and *fear* of the Lord.

This sevenfold ministry of the Holy Spirit is operative in the lives of Christians in a similar way. First, He gives us wisdom and understanding through the Scriptures. Second, He provides us with counsel to direct our lives and might to stand against the onslaughts of Satanic opposition. Finally, He makes known to us the knowledge of Christ (Jn. 15:26; 16:15) and produces in us a reverential respect for God.

Second, the Holy Spirit executes a threefold purpose on earth. He convinces the world of sin, righteousness, and judgment. He reveals the sin of unbelief as being the issue that separates the unsaved from God (Jn. 16:9). He makes known the righteousness of God in Christ to the world (Jn. 16:10). The Holy Spirit convinces the unsaved world of God's judgment on everyone who rejects the saving power of Jesus Christ (Jn. 16:11).

Third, the Holy Spirit plays a major role in our salvation and service for God. In the parable of the ten virgins (Mt. 25:1–13), oil is a symbol of the indwelling Spirit of God. Five wise virgins had oil in their lamps, enabling them to enter into the marriage of the Lord, but five foolish virgins were shut out of the marriage because they had no oil. Only those who have the oil of the Holy Spirit possess true faith in Jesus Christ (Rom. 8:9). All believers are born of the Spirit (Jn. 3:3–6), baptized into the body of Christ (1 Cor. 12:12–13), blessed with gifts for service (1 Cor. 12:7–11, 27–30; Eph. 4:11), and empowered to witness for their Lord (Acts 1:8) through the indwelling power of the Holy Spirit.

Today, the light of the Holy Spirit does not dwell in a temple made with hands but in Christians. Paul wrote, "Know ye not that your body is the temple of the Holy Spirit who is in you" (1 Cor. 6:19). It is the indwelling Spirit whose light makes the teachings of Christ real to us, conforming us to His image (Rom. 8:29).

The lampstand cast its light on the other two pieces of furniture in the holy place, speaking of the Spirit's ministry on our behalf. The light illuminated the table of showbread, from which the priests received daily sustenance. The Holy Spirit illumines Christ, the living Word (Jn. 1:1, 4), and the written Word of God (Jn. 14:16; 16:15) to believers. It is only through the Spirit's ministry that Christians are able to understand the Scriptures (1 Cor. 1:10–14) and receive nourishment from them.

The light from the lampstand also illuminated the altar of incense, so that the priests could see to offer the incense of prayer to God. Without the lighted lampstand, the priests would have worshiped in darkness. For our prayers to be effective, they must be offered in the Spirit (Eph. 6:18). The Holy Spirit takes our unintelligible, insufficient, and feeble prayers to the throne of God and expresses our needs properly, according to the will of God (Rom. 8:26–27).

The Lampstand and Cleansing

→ stretch - trimmed
wick = living
afresh w/ HS
every day - cannot
live in past

The tongs and snuff dishes used in trimming the lampstand are typical of the cleansing of believers. Daily the priests removed any dead material from the wick that might prevent the light from shining brightly. Christians are the wick of God, standing between the oil and the light. When the light is shining brightly, the wick is not seen, but if the light goes out, only the black charred wick is noticed. If our wick is defective, the oil of the Holy Spirit is unable to flow through us, causing the light of Christ to flicker dimly and finally die out. Christians must continually be trimmed by chastening (Heb. 12:5–11), which purges out the deadness of the old life (Jn. 15:1) and allows the light of Christ to beam brightly into the sin-darkened world. Christ, our high priest, trims our wick through the trying of our faith.

The priests placed the used portions of wick into a snuff dish and carried them out of the Tabernacle for proper disposal. The Lord disposes of our purged sins far from His holy presence (Ps. 103:12).

We are commanded to be filled with the oil of the Holy Spirit (Eph. 5:18), so that our light will shine on people in our world. When unconfessed sin remains in our lives, we grieve the Spirit (Eph. 4:30–31), and His ministry is quenched, causing our light to shine dimly or even be extinguished. When we are burning brightly for Christ, we are not seen, but His glory shines through us.

A simple little song sums up the responsibility we have as lights for Christ:

Be a light for Jesus, Brightly shine each day;
    Radiate the Savior, in the home, at play.
Others soon will see it, As you onward go;
    Keep on burning brightly, With a steady glow.

Never let it flicker, Never let it dim;
    Trim your lamp for Jesus, Let it shine for Him.
Shine on thru the darkness, Precious in God's sight,
    Are His own dear children, Walking in His light.

Are you a bright light shining over the dark sea of humanity, pointing people to Christ, the true haven of rest? Only you can answer how brightly your light is shining for our Lord.

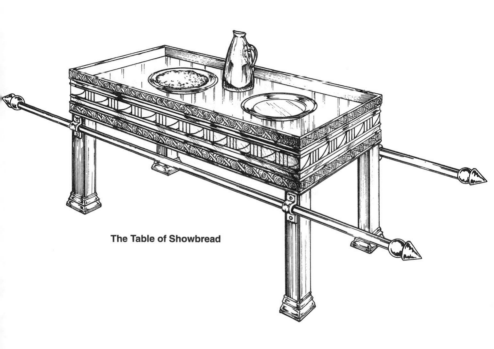

The Table of Showbread

Thou shalt also make a table of acacia wood: two cubits shall be the length thereof, and a cubit the breadth thereof, and a cubit and a half the height thereof. And thou shalt overlay it with pure gold, and make thereto a rim of gold round about. And thou shalt make unto it a border of an handbreadth round about, and thou shalt make a golden rim to the border thereof round about. And thou shalt make for it four rings of gold, and put the rings in the four corners that are on the four feet thereof.

Exodus 25:23–26

CHAPTER 5

The Table of Showbread

(Exodus 25:23–30; Leviticus 24:5–9)

Light from the golden lampstand illuminated the table of showbread, causing it to sparkle with dazzling beauty as the small, ornately tooled table stately stood on the right side of the holy place.

Moses had instructed the Spirit-filled craftsman how to construct the table of showbread. It was made of shittim (acacia) wood covered with gold. A gold rim encircled its top; gold rings were placed at each corner; and acacia wood staves covered with gold were placed through the rings to carry it. The table was three feet long, one and a half feet wide, and two and three-tenths feet high (Ex. 25:23–28). Serving vessels of pure gold were provided to minister at the table (Ex. 25:29). Dishes (bread pans) were made for carrying the bread into the holy place. The spoons (incense cups) were filled with frankincense, which was poured on top of the bread and burned on the altar of incense (Lev. 24:7; Num. 7:14). The covers (flagons) and bowls (cups) were used in the drink offering that accompanied the meal offering in the Tabernacle (Lev. 23:18; Num. 6:15).

The Structure of the Table

The table of showbread typified the Lord's life and ministry. Shittim (acacia) wood is a hard, incorruptible, indestructible wood that grows in the Sinai Desert. As we saw with the brazen altar, it typified the humanity of Christ, who came as a root out of dry ground (Isa. 53:2) and was sinless in His human nature (Heb. 4:15; 7:26). The indestructibility of the wood spoke of Christ in His humanity, withstanding the fire of crucifixion (Jn. 10:18), the decaying effect of the grave (Acts 2:31), and His bodily resurrection (Mt. 28:5–6).

The gold in the table was emblematic of Jesus' deity. The Bible explicitly states that Jesus is divine (Jn. 1:1; 10:30–33; 20:28), ascribing such divine attributes to Him as His eternal existence (Rev. 1:8), omnipresence (Mt. 28:20), omniscience (Jn. 2:24–25), and omnipotence (Phil. 3:21).

The table of wood overlaid with gold typified the union of Jesus' divine and human natures (Phil. 2:6–11). The Scriptures teach that He had two natures, but we cannot ascribe two personalities to Him. The union of His divine and human natures should never be thought of in terms of deity possessing humanity, which would deny His humanity. Neither should we think that His humanity was simply indwelt by deity. Jesus was uniquely different from any other man who ever walked the face of the earth; both His divine and human natures were united together in one person. This teaching is clearly set forth in the Scriptures but is difficult for some people to grasp.

The Showbread on the Table

The fragrance of freshly baked bread topped with frankincense filled the holy place. Twelve new cakes of bread containing about six pounds of flour were arranged in two rows of six loaves each. It is not stated in the Scripture that the bread was unleavened, but because it was a meal offering to be used in the Tabernacle, it had to have been unleavened bread.

The changing of the showbread was an elaborate service. The Mishna (the first section of the Talmud) explains the procedure the priests used in changing the bread.

Four priests entered the holy place, two of them carrying the piles of bread, and two of them the cups of incense. Four priests had gone in before them, two to take off the two old piles of showbread, and two to take off the cups of incense. Those who brought in the new bread stood at the north side facing southward, those who took away the old bread, at the south side, facing northward. One part lifted off and the other put on, the hands of one being over against the hands of the other, as it is written, 'Thou shalt set upon the table bread of the Passover always before me' (Men. XI, 7). The loaves that were removed were delivered to the priests for their consumption within the Tabernacle, the whole quantity amounting to seventy-five pounds of bread per week.

The term *showbread* comes from a Hebrew word that means *bread of the face* or *bread of presence*, because the loaves were set before the face or presence of Jehovah (who dwelt in the holy of holies) as a meal offering from the children of Israel (Lev. 24:8). God gazed with delight on the pure bread offering that sat continually before His face. Bread is called the staff of life and is emblematic of life itself. The showbread was a foreshadowing of Jesus Christ, who is the true bread of life, giving unfailing sustenance to all who partake of Him. He was born in the city of Bethlehem which means *house of bread*.

Jesus is pictured as the bread of life in many places throughout the Scriptures. In John 6 He is referred to as the bread of life who came down from heaven to give life to everyone who accepts Him. The day before He revealed Himself as the bread of life, Jesus performed the miracle of multiplying a young boy's five barley loaves into enough bread to feed 5,000 men. After the meal, 12 full baskets of bread remained (Jn. 6:1–14). The next day the people who had been fed followed Jesus to Capernaum, hoping that He would provide more food for them. They sought Him only for the material benefits He was able to provide (Jn. 6:22–26), rather than because of the miracle He had performed.

Knowing their hearts, Jesus made a comparison between natural food, which gave only temporary satisfaction, and the spiritual food He provided to bring permanent satisfaction. Misunderstanding His statement, the people believed they had to do some outward work to acquire eternal life. Jesus replied that it was not the keeping of external ordinances and laws that provided eternal life; rather, eternal life came through believing in Him (Jn. 6:27–29).

Completely discounting the first miracle, the people required a sign from Jesus to validate His claim of being able to provide eternal life. Using the context of the multiplication of the bread, they gave the illustration of Moses, who provided bread from heaven for their forefathers in the wilderness. They reasoned that if Jesus was a prophet from God with authority to give eternal life, certainly He would be able to produce convincing evidence, such as Moses did when he provided manna from heaven. Jesus corrected their assumption that Moses had given their fathers bread. He instead gave God the Father credit for providing the manna. Again, Jesus emphasized that He alone is the true bread from God who will give eternal life to all who believe (Jn. 6:30–33). Jesus then made a startling statement: "I am the living bread that came down from heaven; if any man eat of this bread, he shall live forever; and the bread that I will give is my flesh, which I will give for the life of the world" (Jn. 6:51).

The metaphor "eat of this bread" did not teach the necessity of literally eating the flesh of Jesus to acquire eternal life. Jesus simply taught that as food becomes part of an individual as it is consumed, so all who believe in Him as the one who gives life are completely assimilating Him. Jesus illustrated this point by comparing it with His relationship with the Father. As He and God the Father dwell together in oneness (Jn. 6:57), so will true believers be indwelt by Him (Jn. 6:56).

The showbread typified Christ's sinless life. The Mosaic law strictly forbade leaven, a symbol of sin (Ex. 12:8, 15–20; Mt. 16:6), from being used in the flour set aside for priestly ritual (Lev. 2:11). Jesus, the bread of life, was without sin (2 Cor. 5:21; 1 Pet. 1:19).

The showbread was produced from fine flour (Lev. 2:1), which speaks of the evenness and uniformity of the Lord's life and ministry. To make grain into fine flour, it must be crushed, ground, and sifted. What a picture of the Lord's ministry! Jesus went through the sifting process of Satan's temptation (Mt. 4:1–11) and the religious leaders' testing (Mt. 22:15–40), yet no sin was found in Him (Heb. 4:15). He went through the crushing experiences of scourging (Isa. 53:4–5; Mt. 27:26–30) and crucifixion (Mt. 27:33–50) for the sin of mankind.

Nature provided a parable for the purpose of Jesus' coming. In John 12:24, Jesus pictured His life as a grain of wheat that must die to produce fruit. The grain falls into the ground and dies, but through its death the life of that single grain is freed from its encasement to regenerate itself into thousands of other grains possessing the same nature. Through death, Jesus brought resurrection life to all who will put their faith in His finished work on the cross.

The refined flour was baked into loaves, another picture of Jesus, who went through the fire of persecution, suffering, and death for us. Peter stated it well when he wrote, "For Christ also hath once suffered for sins, the just for the unjust, that he might bring us to God, being put to death in the flesh but made alive by the Spirit" (1 Pet. 3:18).

After the loaves were placed on the table, they were sprinkled with frankincense as a memorial, and the remainder was burned on the altar of incense as an offering to Jehovah (Lev. 24:7). The frankincense should not be confused with the regular incense burned on the altar; it was different in substance. Frankincense is a fragrant gum resin with a silvery white cast. It was ground into powder and burned on the altar while the priests ate the showbread on the Sabbath. The incense emitted a balsam-like fragrance that filled the holy place.

The frankincense typified Christ in two ways. First, at Jesus' birth one of the wise men presented Him with frankincense (Mt. 2:11), emblematic of the fragrance of His life. The incense pictures the Lord's life as He manifested the sweet fragrance of perfection in all that He said and did. Second, the incense is symbolic of Christ living through the lives of Christians. Paul said, "Now thanks be unto

God, who always causeth us to triumph in Christ, and maketh manifest the savor of his knowledge by us in every place. For we are unto God a sweet savor of Christ" (2 Cor. 2:14–15).

The Service at the Table

The loaves were gathered from the 12 tribes each Sabbath and used in two ways. First, they were brought as a unit by the 12 tribes as a portion of their labor to be dedicated to the Lord's service each week. Paul typified this in the church when he wrote, "For we being many are one bread, and one body; for we are all partakers of that one bread" (1 Cor. 10:17). As one bread in the Lord, we are to give sustenance to one another by exercising our gifts within the church (1 Cor. 12:12–17).

By bringing their bread offering to the Lord each Sabbath, the Israelites symbolized Christian giving. Paul instructed us to systematically set aside a portion of our income as God has prospered us, and, through our local church, we are to present our tithes to the Lord on the first day of the week (1 Cor. 16:2).

Second, the bread provided food to be eaten by the priests on the Sabbath in the holy place (Lev. 24:5–9). We, as believer-priests (1 Pet. 2:9), are to feed on Christ, the bread of life, receiving in return spiritual sustenance and strength for worship and service. Jesus is the source of our spiritual vitality and fruitfulness in service. He said, "without me you can do nothing" (Jn. 15:5). Paul saw our great need for Christ when he wrote, "I can do all things through Christ, who strengtheneth me" (Phil. 4:13).

The bread and wine that sat on the table of showbread spoke of the priests' fellowship with the Lord. Our communion with the Lord typifies fellowship as well. On the first day of the week, we gather as a body of believers to have communion with our Lord around the table. We partake of bread and the fruit of the vine in remembrance of Jesus' broken body and death on the cross on our behalf (1 Cor. 11:23–26).

Today, many Christians are spiritually starving. Some attend churches that only feed them the humanistic, philosophic opinions of the world. Others attend churches that feed them the husk of spiritual experience without sound teaching from the Word of God. Jesus stands knocking at the door of our lives asking for admission. He wants to feed us the spiritual bread of God's Word, which can edify us for service.

We should not be content to just feast on the spiritual sustenance that Christ provides with no concern for others. We must look around us at the hungry souls who are starving for lack of spiritual food and provide sustenance for them. If you were the only one in your neighborhood with food, could you, in good conscience, fill yourself while others around you were starving? Of course you couldn't! God has commanded us to take Christ, the bread of life, to those around us so that their spiritual appetites can be satisfied.

The hymn writer summed up what every Christian should desire:

> Guide me, O Thou great Jehovah,
>   Pilgrim through this barren land;
> I am week, but Thou art mighty;
>   Hold me with Thy powerful hand;
> Bread of heaven, Bread of heaven,
>   Feed me till I want no more,
> Feed me till I want no more.

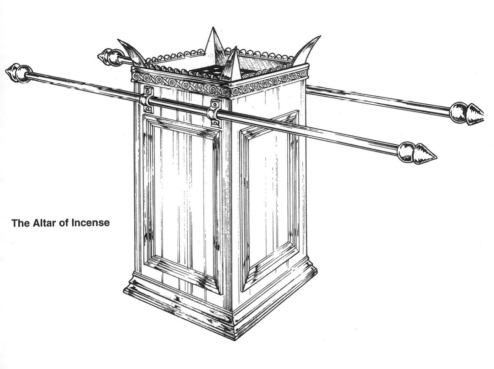

The Altar of Incense

And thou shalt make an altar to burn incense upon: of acacia wood shalt thou make it. A cubit shall be the length thereof, and a cubit the breadth thereof; foursquare shall it be: and the two cubits shall be the height thereof; the horns thereof shall be of the same. And thou shalt overlay it with pure gold, the top thereof, and the sides thereof round about, and the horns thereof; and thou shalt make unto it a rim of gold round about. And two golden rings shalt thou make to it under the rim of it, by the two corners thereof, upon the two sides of it shalt thou make it; and they shall be for places for the staves with which to bear it.

Exodus 30:1–4

CHAPTER 6

The Altar of Incense

(Exodus 30:1–10; 34–38)

Τhe sun was rising over the horizon as the priest entered the holy place to trim the lampstand and offer sweet incense on the golden altar. He never minimized his high holy privilege of serving in the Tabernacle. He alone was the mediator who offered intercessory prayer before a holy God on behalf of the nation of Israel.

The priest took a censer full of burning coals from the brazen altar in one hand and specially prepared sweet incense in the other hand and ignited the incense by sprinkling it over the burning coals (Lev. 16:12–13). A thick cloud of smoke curled upward filling the Tabernacle, symbolic of Israel's prayers to God. The priest, enveloped by the sweet fragrance of the cloudy incense, must have been lifted to inexpressible heights of blessing as he communed with God in this sanctified place.

The Pattern for the Altar

The golden altar of incense, which was 36 inches high and 18 inches square, was much smaller than the brazen altar. It was made of acacia wood, covered with gold, and had a horn at each corner. A gold rim encircled the top with gold rings at each corner, and acacia wood staves covered with gold were put through the rings to transport it (Ex. 30:1–6).

Earlier we noted that acacia wood covered with gold was a picture of Christ's humanity and deity wedded into one person. John expressed that union beautifully when he wrote, "And the Word was made flesh, and dwelt among us (and we beheld his glory, the glory as of the only begotten of the Father), full of grace and truth" (Jn. 1:14). The very God of the universe took on flesh and joined Himself to sinful humanity so that through His shed blood we might have our sins forgiven and be reconciled to God (2 Cor. 5:18–19, 21; Heb. 2:14–17).

The Placement of the Altar

Placing the altar before the veil (Ex. 30:6) was of great significance. The golden altar stood next to the veil in the center of the holy place, which separated it from the holy of holies where God manifested His presence. Thus, the closest the priests could come to God in daily worship was when they ministered at the altar of incense.

The same principle holds true for Christians. The closest we can come to God is through prayer (Jas. 4:8). There is a significant difference between the way we come to God and the way the Aaronic priests came to Him. Today, there is no veil separating us from the throne of God, as there was in the Tabernacle. The veil was rent at the crucifixion of the Lord, giving us direct access to the throne of God through the veil of Christ's flesh and by way of His shed blood (Heb. 10:19–20). The golden altar of incense stands before the throne of God (Rev. 8:3) as an everlasting testimony to the prayers of believers as they ascend into His presence.

The Preparation of the Incense

The incense was made from three specific sweet perfumes (Ex. 30:34) mixed with frankincense: Stacte, which was either a sweet gum that exuded from the storax tree (similar to a poplar tree) growing in Israel or a few drops of myrrh; onycha (Heb., shell), which comes from the shell of a mollusk and, when burned, gives off a perfumed fragrance; and galbanum, a gum resin that emits a milky sap with a balsamic odor and comes from the Syrian fennel. Frankincense is a fragrant white gum that comes from a tree called the salai found in Arabia. The spices were weighed out equally (Ex. 30:34), mixed into one substance by the perfumers (Ex. 30:35), and beaten to emit their fragrances (Ex. 30:36).

The sweet smelling incense was a beautiful picture of Christ in all His perfection and grace before God and mankind. His life emitted a fragrant perfection of purity and holiness unmarred by sin or fleshly motives. Christians are called "a sweet savor" to God and the world (2 Cor. 2:14–16). As we move through society, we are like incense that has been crushed and burned, emitting the perfume of the knowledge of Christ to the glory of God. The world responds in various ways to Christians as they emit the fragrance of Christ. To those who are lost and indifferent to the gospel, the incense of Christ is "the savor of death unto death; but to those who respond to our witness, Christ is "the savor of life unto life." Some of the incense was beaten and put before the testimony (ark of the covenant) in the Tabernacle outside the holy of holies (Ex. 30:36), ready to be used when necessary. So it is with Christians, whose hearts should be prepared before God to offer up the sweet incense of prayer.

The Priests' Preparation for Intercessory Prayer

Before the priests could offer the incense of prayer, three requirements had to be met. First, the priests had to minister at the brazen altar, shedding the blood of an animal for their sins. Before we are able to come before a holy God in prayer, we must be cleansed by the shed blood of Jesus Christ, which is done by appropriating His sacrificial death on the cross on our behalf.

Second, the priests had to wash all defilement from their hands and feet (Ex. 30:18–20) before they could enter the holy place to offer the ministry of prayer. We must confess our sins and come before God with clean hearts before He will hear our prayers. Unconfessed sin in the lives of believers hampers God from listening and responding to their prayers (1 Jn. 1:6–10). As believer-priests, we are to be set apart unto holiness. Third, the priests had to be in the holy place to offer the incense of prayer. Cleansed by blood and water, they stepped into the sanctuary to fellowship with God. The writer of Hebrews summed it up well when he said, "Let us draw near with a true heart in full assurance of faith, having our hearts sprinkled from an evil conscience, and our bodies washed with pure water" (Heb. 10:22). It is only when we are in a proper relationship with God that we can have the full assurance that He will answer our prayers.

The Priests' Participation in Intercessory Prayer

Aaron was to offer incense on the golden altar at regular times each day (Ex. 30:7–8). When the priests offered the morning and evening sacrifices on the brazen altar, they also entered the holy place to trim the golden lampstand and burn incense on the altar. In New Testament times, the disciples kept morning and evening hours of prayer in the Temple and in their homes (Acts 3:1; 10:9, 30), indicating that God desires believers to set aside specific times for prayer throughout the day.

Many wonder when is the best time to pray—in the morning or evening? Although the Lord does not stipulate a set time for Christians to pray, the biblical pattern is that we should pray both morning and evening. We should offer morning prayers of praise and petition, inviting to Lord to give us direction as we begin the day. The Bible is full of examples of those who rose early in the morning for prayer: Samuel's parents (1 Sam. 1:19); Hezekiah (2 Chr. 29:20); Job (Job 1:5); David (Ps. 57:8); and Jesus (Mk. 1:35). In the evening we should reflect on the day, thanking and praising God for answered prayer and the direction He gave us. David found great solace and strength when he meditated in prayer in the quietness of the night watches (Ps. 63:5–6). At times the Lord spent whole nights in prayer (Lk. 6:12).

The incense burned perpetually before the Lord throughout the years (Ex. 30:8), picturing believers offering up prayers continually to God. Paul instructed us to "Pray without ceasing" (1 Th. 5:17), meaning that we are to be in a continual attitude of prayer throughout the day. This was exemplified by the Lord (Heb. 7:25) and the Holy Spirit (Rom. 8:26–27), who perpetually intercede for us before the throne of God the Father.

The prepared incense was burned with fire by the priests: "And he shall put the incense upon the fire before the LORD" (Lev. 16:13). The same fire that consumed the sacrifice on the brazen altar was used to consume the incense. This, too, is a picture of Christ. Because He experienced the fires of suffering and sacrifice to secure our salvation, He is able to appear in heaven as our advocate, making it possible for us to have direct access to God through prayer (Heb. 9:24; 1 Jn. 2:1–2). Calvary gives validity to our prayers.

Two solemn warnings were given concerning the type of incense and fire that could be used on the golden altar. First, no strange incense could be used on the altar (Ex. 30:9), nor could anyone make the incense for his own personal use (Ex. 30:37). Anyone who did so was "cut off from his people" (put to death) [Ex. 30:38]. This is a figure of prayer offered contrary to God's will. Our prayer life is to conform to the pattern set forth by God in His Word. We are not to offer prayer through "vain repetitions" (Mt. 6:7) but after the model presented by the Lord when His disciples asked Him to teach them to pray (Lk. 11:1–4). Our prayers should always be offered in the divine will of God (1 Jn. 5:14–15) by the authority of Jesus' name (Jn. 14:13). Our prayers are hindered when we are out of fellowship with God, harbor an unforgiving spirit against a brother in Christ (Mt. 6:15), or pray selfishly out of the will of God (Jas. 4:3).

Second, no fire other than that from the brazen altar could be used on the golden altar. When Nadab and Abihu offered strange fire, they immediately died by the hand of the Lord (Lev. 10:1–2). These men were true priests with true incense, but they used fire that had not been prescribed by God (Lev. 6:12–13; 16:12). They willfully disobeyed God's expressed command concerning worship at the golden altar. Some may question the harsh judgment from God on these two priests, but it is a grim reminder of the fact that rebellion against the expressed will of God can bring His judgment even on believers. It also illustrates that we should not worship and serve God according to the flesh but according to His revealed will in the Scriptures.

The horns of the altar of incense were not just for decoration but served a specific purpose in relationship to the blood sacrifice. First, on the day of atonement (the tenth day of the seventh month), the high priest took some of the blood that was used to sprinkle the mercy seat and put it on the horns of the altar of incense to "make an atonement upon the horns of it" (Ex. 30:10). The purpose of this act was to "cleanse it, and hallow it from the uncleanness of the children of Israel" (Lev. 16:18–19).

Second, the altar served as a place of expiation for the sins of the priests and the congregation (Lev. 4:7–8, 18). The sin offering was a compulsory offering covering sins committed unintentionally, in contrast to those committed premeditatively out of rebellion to God's commandments. It typifies Christ, who was made sin for us. Paul wrote, "For he hath made him, who knew no sin, to be sin for us, that we might be made the righteousness of God in him" (2 Cor. 5:21). The sin offering had three purposes: It acted as a substitute for the sins of individuals; its blood was efficacious in atoning for sin; and the application of the blood expiated sin (freed individuals from the punishment of sin).

The golden altar also represented the place of intercession before the Lord; thus, when blood from the sin offering was sprinkled on the horns of the altar, it symbolized a prayer for the pardon of sin before God. The blood, when applied to the altar, gave the incense of prayer its value. So it is with Christ's blood, which gives value to our prayers before God (Heb. 9:14; 12:24) and opens the way for us to come before the throne of grace to find mercy and grace in the time of need (Heb. 4:16).

As was already stated, the priests interceded before the Lord on behalf of the people, giving a beautiful picture of the Lord's intercession on behalf of believers. The Bible clearly states that He "ever liveth to make intercession for them" (Heb. 7:25). Just before the Lord's betrayal, He gave an example (recorded in John 17) of the type of intercession He offers on behalf of believers. There is no reason to doubt that He continues to pray the same prayer in heaven today. In His prayer, He asked the Father to provide a number of things for believers: protection from the world (v. 11), protection from Satan (v. 15), sanctification through the Scripture (v. 17), spiritual unity within the body of Christ (vv. 21–23), and the presence of believers with Him to behold His glory (v. 24).

The Privilege of Prayer

Moses ended his description of the golden altar and its ministry by calling it "most holy unto the LORD" (Ex. 30:10). Next to the ark of the covenant, it was the most sacred piece of furniture in the Tabernacle, illustrating the tremendous importance God puts on our communion with Him in prayer.

Christian friend, do you cherish the high holy privilege that is yours to enter the throne room of God and converse with Him in prayer? Sad to say, this important privilege is often minimized in our walk with their Lord. God has much to say concerning prayer. He has made it clear that prayer should be a priority in our lives. We are commanded to "Pray without ceasing" (1 Th. 5:17). We are not to become weary: "men ought always to pray, and not to faint" (Lk. 18:1). We are to pray in order to strengthen ourselves against the destructive onslaught of Satan: "Watch ye and pray, lest ye enter into temptation" (Mk. 14:38). Without prayer, Christians become spiritually weak and eventually powerless in their walk before the Lord and testimony before others.

William W. Walford was a blind English preacher of lowly birth. Although he did not possess a formal education, people called him "the walking Bible" because of his ability to quote Scripture with great preciseness. Although he was unable to see the beauty of this world, the glories of heaven were opened to him through the privilege of prayer. Spending many sweet hours in the throne room of intercessory prayer, he was moved to pen these words in 1842:

> Sweet hour of prayer, sweet hour of prayer,
> > That calls me from a world of care,
> And bids me at my Father's throne
> > Make all my wants and wishes known:
>
> In seasons of distress and grief,
> > My soul has often found relief,
> And oft escaped the tempter's snare,
> > By thy return, sweet hour of prayer.

Why not take the next hour and taste the sweetness that an hour of prayer will bring to your life? If you do, you and those around you will savor a fresh fragrance of God's peace and power flowing from your life.

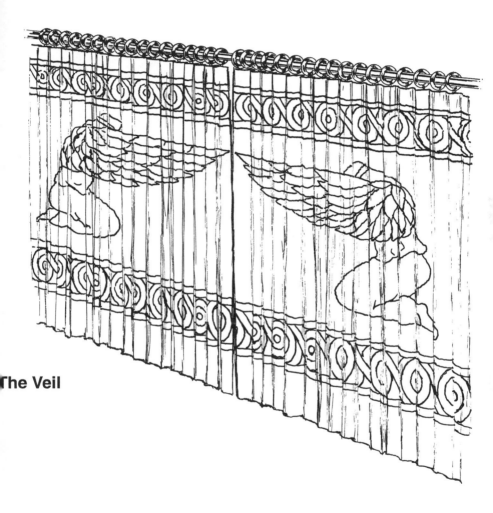

The Veil

And thou shalt make a veil of blue, and purple, and scarlet, and fine-twined linen of skillful work; with cherubim shall it be made: And thou shalt hang it upon four pillars of acacia wood overlaid with gold: their hooks shall be of gold, upon the four sockets of silver. And thou shalt hang up the veil under the clasps, that thou mayest bring in thither within the veil the ark of the testimony: and the veil shall divide unto you between the holy place and the most holy.

Exodus 26:31–33

CHAPTER 7

The Veil

(Exodus 26:31–35; 36:35–38)

The multicolored veil embroidered with images of cherubim hung elegantly between the holy place and the holy of holies, separating the priest from God's glorious presence. The images of cherubim gazing on the movements of the ministering priest made him aware of the holiness of his office.

What must have gone through his mind as he looked at the beautiful veil? Did he think, What would it be like to enter the veil? Would I really die if I entered? Why not take just a peek into the holy of holies? The convicting answer from his conscience was, No! Don't! He vividly remembered how quickly judgment from God fell upon Nadab and Abihu when they were disobedient in their ministry.

Placement of the Curtains

Three curtains were placed strategically in the Tabernacle, each one made of fine-twined linen into which twisted threads of blue, purple, and scarlet were interwoven (Ex. 38:18). Although beautiful to the eye, the veiled entrances of the

Tabernacle were not to be objects of admiration; rather, they performed two basic functions. The word *veil* (Heb., *paroketh*) means to *separate* and describes its ministry. The veil acted as a barrier between God and man, shutting God in and man out (Lev. 16:2), and the curtains permitted access to worship after the priests had met the required conditions set forth in the Mosaic law.

The first curtain, "the gate of the court" (Ex. 27:16), was seven and a half feet high and 30 feet wide and was supported by four pillars set in bronze sockets. This curtain separated the people from the Tabernacle court. They brought their sacrifice to the gate as an offering to God. The second curtain, the "hanging for the door of the tent" (Ex. 26:36–37), was supported by five pillars with gold hooks. The five pillars were made of acacia wood overlaid with gold and were fastened to the pillars with the gold hooks that were attached to the five bronze sockets. This curtain separated the priests in the Tabernacle court from the holy place. Only after cleansing at the brazen altar and the brazen laver could the priests enter the holy place to worship and fellowship with God.

The third veil, the one being focused on in this chapter, divided the inside of the Tabernacle into two rooms, the holy place and the holy of holies. It hung from gold hooks supported by four pillars of acacia wood overlaid with gold anchored into four sockets of silver (Ex. 36:31–33). This veil separated the priests from the holy of holies, where the presence of God dwelt. Only the high priest could enter the holy of holies once a year, on the day of atonement, to offer blood on the mercy seat for his sins and those of the people.

The veil between the holy place and the holy of holies is described as a "skillful work" (Ex. 26:31). The workers were given special divine wisdom in the making of this beautiful veil, which has never been duplicated.

The awesome figures of the cherubim woven into the veil were images of angelic beings of the highest order. Their character, beauty, and power surpass human description. Symbols of cherubim were used by other Semitic people, appearing in the likeness of winged lions and bulls, to guard their temples and palaces. Ezekiel gave the impression that cherubim have both the characteristics of men and animals (Ezek. 10). Cherubim are symbolic of God's protective presence over the holy of holies. It was as if God had placed a continuous guard before its entrance saying, "Thus far, but no further!" They were placed at the entrance of the Garden of Eden after Adam and Eve were driven out to protect the tree of life (Gen. 3:24). The veil that hung in Herod's Temple during the Lord's day was beautiful to behold, according to Jewish tradition. There were actually two veils in front of the holy of holies. The Talmud states that it was not known whether the veil in Solomon's Temple hung inside or outside the entrance to the holy of holies (Yoma 51). According to Maimonides, there was no wall between the holy place and the holy of holies, but a space of one cubit (about 18 inches) was assigned to it where the veil was hung. Since the priests in Herod's time did not know on which side of the cubit the veil was hung, they hung two veils, one nearer the holy place and the other nearer the holy of holies.

According to the Talmud, the veils were 60 feet long and 30 feet wide, about the thickness of a man's palm (four inches), and made of 72 squares that were sown together. The veils were so heavy that it took 300 priests to hang them, according to Jewish tradition.

During the time of Herod's Temple, the high priest entered three times on the day of atonement. First, he entered with a censer of hot coals in one hand and incense in the other. The light of the hot coals faintly illuminated the empty room of the holy of holies, casting a shadowy red glow throughout the room. The shekinah cloud of God's glory filled the holy of holies in Solomon's Temple, but that glory had departed (Ezek. 10:18; 11:23). The ark of the covenant had been removed at the time the Temple was destroyed by the Babylonians. Sprinkling incense on the hot coals, the high priest watched as it was consumed, filling the room with its cloudy fragrance. Next, the high priest took the blood of a freshly slain bullock and entered the holy of holies to sprinkle it upward one time, where the ark of the covenant once stood, and downward seven times, counting as he did so in order not to make a mistake. Finally, the high priest took a he-goat,

killed it, and entered a third time, offering its blood in the holy of
holies just as he had done with the bullock's blood.

Provision Through Christ

The veil was a graphic picture of the Lord's life and ministry. As
the veil in the Tabernacle hid the glory of God, so the divine glory
of God was hidden during His earthly ministry (Jn. 1:1, 14, 18).
Paul wrote, "Who, being in the form of God, thought it not robbery to be equal with God, But made himself of no reputation, and
took upon him the form of a servant, and was made in the likeness
of men" (Phil. 2:6–7). Christ, who is of the same nature and
essence of God, emptied Himself, or took on the limitations of
humanity without surrendering any of His attributes as deity. He
voluntarily allowed the limitation of some of His divine rights
during His earthly ministry. Jesus illustrated this in reference to
His Second Coming when He said, "But of that day and hour
knoweth no man, no, not the angels of heaven, but my Father
only" (Mt. 24:36). At one point in His ministry, He revealed His
glory to a few disciples when He was transfigured before them
(Mt. 17:2). At other times, glimpses of His glory were seen through
the various miracles He performed (Jn. 2:11; 11:40). Christ's glory
was restored after His resurrection (Jn. 17:5, 24).

The colorful materials used to make the veil are typical of
Christ's ministry. The fine-twined linen was an Egyptian white
byssus yarn woven tightly together (twice as good as the quality
of linen produced by modern technology). The white speaks of
purity and righteousness. The fineness denotes the faultlessness
of the material. These materials provide another picture of Christ,
who, in His flesh, was without blemish and spot (1 Pet. 1:19). The
fine white linen is also a type of the saints of God who will be
arrayed in fine white linen garments at the marriage of the Lamb,
symbolizing their righteousness before Him (Rev. 19:7–8).

The three colors woven into the veil are symbolic of Christ's
incarnation, ministry, and second advent. The blue, probably
indigo, was produced from a species of shellfish and speaks of
Christ's coming down from heaven as the Son of God to do the

Father's will (Jn. 3:13, 31; 8:23; Acts 1:11). Scarlet was a bright red dye produced from worms or grubs and provides a vivid picture of Christ's ministry in shedding His blood to purchase our salvation (Rom. 3:25; 5:9). The purple was produced from a secretion of the purple snail (murex). Purple is the color of royalty and speaks of Christ's kingship. Jesus was from the kingly line of David (Lk. 1:32), born a King (Mt. 2:2), mocked as a King (Mt. 27:29), declared to be King at His crucifixion (Mt. 27:37), and is coming back as the King of kings and Lord of lords (Rev. 19:16) to rule as King forever (Lk. 1:33).

Before the rending of the veil, mankind had no direct access into God's presence. But in a simplistic yet profound act, God tore away the barrier that had separated Him from sinful humanity for more than 1,500 years. Simultaneously with the death of Jesus Christ, the veil was rent. Matthew wrote, "And, behold, the veil of the temple was torn in two from the top to the bottom; and the earth did quake, and the rocks were split" (Mt. 27:51).

Many critics of the Bible have denied that the tearing of the veil was an act of God, but there is too much evidence to the contrary. Some credit the earthquake that occurred at Christ's crucifixion for rending the veil, but this would have been impossible. The veil may have fallen to the ground during the earthquake, but it would not have been divided down the middle. In addition, the text clearly shows that the earthquake took place after the rending of the veil. If the earthquake had torn the veil, the Temple would have been damaged in the process, and there is no evidence that this happened. Neither is the view that it was hung from a large beam that broke in the middle possible.

Others claim that men tore the veil, but its size and thickness make this claim almost inconceivable. They would have had to tear it from the bottom upward, but the veil was torn from the top downward (Mt. 27:51). Further, the veil was not shredded but torn into two equal halves, showing that it was supernaturally divided.

The rending took place at the time of Jesus' death, the ninth hour (3:00 P.M.) [Mt. 27:45]. At that time, the priests were busy in the Temple preparing the evening sacrifice. Hundreds of people were in the Temple area, and every eye witnessed this miraculous event. Awe and amazement must have struck the priests as they heard and viewed the divine stroke of God tearing the huge veil in half. The empty room of the holy of holies stood wide open before the priests, as if bidding them to come in—a privilege no priest, except the high priest, had enjoyed since the inception of the Tabernacle.

It was at this point that God proclaimed to the Jewish people and the world that the ministration of the Jewish priesthood had ended. No longer was a high priest needed to annually atone for sin. Jesus, the true high priest, had opened the way for mankind to come into the presence of God through His atoning blood (Heb. 6:19; 9:3–15; 10:19).

The torn veil is a picture of the torn body of Christ, who made it possible for us to worship at the throne of God. The same hand that tore the veil in the Temple tore the body of Jesus on our behalf. The writer to the Hebrews stated it well when he said, "Having therefore, brethren, boldness to enter into the holiest by the blood of Jesus, By a new and living way, which he hath consecrated for us, through the veil, that is to say, his flesh" (Heb. 10:19–20). Through His death, Jesus inaugurated (opened for the first time) a way for man to have direct access to God. The word *new*, meaning *newly slain*, describes Jesus' sacrifice. Although His sacrifice for our sins was once and for all performed almost 2,000 years ago, it never grows old but always seems fresh and recent for all who accept it. His shed blood is a continual fountain, cleansing all who appropriate it for their sin. Not only is it new, but it is a living way or a life-giving way. Christ, who is the only way and life (Jn. 14:6), has made it possible for us to enter into God's presence through the veil of His flesh. He changed the veil from a barrier to a gateway.

Privilege for the Christian

For Christians, the rent veil means that we have a mediating high priest (1 Tim. 2:5) who has opened the way for us to have access to the throne of God. It means that we can come at any time into the presence of God with the confidence that we will obtain mercy and find grace to help us in any need we wish to express.

Since we have the high and holy privilege of entering into God's presence, we are exhorted to exercise a fourfold commitment to the Lord, as expressed in Hebrews 10:22–25. First, we are to be cleansed for worship: "Let us draw near with a true heart in full assurance of faith, having our hearts sprinkled from an evil conscience, and our bodies washed with pure water" (Heb. 10:22). We are not to stand far off from God, as the Israelites had to do under the Mosaic Covenant (Num. 18:22) but are, rather, to "draw near." Four conditions must be met before we can come. We are to come with a "true heart," which means more than just coming in sincerity—we are to come in purity and with truthful motives. We are also to come in "full assurance of faith," with the anticipation of appropriating all that God has promised to do for those who come before Him in a right relationship. We are to come "having our hearts sprinkled from an evil conscience, and our bodies washed with pure water," which was typical of the high priest who, before he could approach God, had to be sprinkled with the blood of the sacrifice and wash his body at the laver. Then, and only then, could he enter the holy of holies with a pure conscience before God. We, too, must experience the cleansing power of Christ's blood, freeing us from an evil conscience of sin, so that we can come into God's presence with bold confidence in our worship.

Second, we are exhorted to have a confession before the world: "Let us hold fast the profession of our faith without wavering (for he is faithful that promised)" (Heb. 10:23). We are not to waver (lit., bend) in our faith (lit., hope) under the fire of persecution. We should not rely on our own strength but on God's, who said, "I will never leave thee, nor forsake thee" (Heb. 13:5). God has promised that He will never abandon us under any circumstance; thus, we can take great comfort and encouragement in God's precious promises, which give us the strength to stand with a consistent life before a world that opposes our faith.

Third, we are to exhort others to a life of commitment in the work: "And let us consider one another to provoke unto love and to good works" (Heb. 10:24). We are to continuously care for the spiritual welfare of fellow Christians, to provide (lit., stimulate) them to lives of love and good works in their walk before the world and fellow believers. In love we are to stir up one another to exercise the spiritual gifts that have been given to us by the Holy Spirit.

Fourth, we are exhorted not to forsake corporate worship: "Not forsaking the assembling of ourselves together, as the manner of some is, but exhorting one another, and so much the more, as ye see the day approaching" (Heb. 10:25). We are not to abandon the local church, as many will do in the latter days. On the contrary, we are to exhort one another to continue attending, especially when we know that the Lord's coming is very near.

Believers have the glorious privilege of approaching God directly. But perhaps you, like many in the church, have erected the veil of cooling commitment, faulty faith, lost love for the Lord, slackness of service for the Savior, or forsaken fellowship with the family of God.

Judson W. VanDeVenter had erected a veil. But while singing in a choir during a revival campaign in Sharon, Pennsylvania, he responded to the invitation and committed his life to the Lord's service. He forsook all and became an evangelist, ministering in America, England, and Scotland. Years later he wrote about his commitment:

All to Jesus I surrender,
    All to Him I freely give;
I will ever love and trust Him,
    In His presence daily live.

All to Jesus I surrender,
    Lord, I give myself to Thee;
Fill me with Thy love and power,
    Let Thy blessing fall on me.

The Lord stands ready to tear away the veil of division. He bids you to come in commitment to Him. Why not do like Judson VanDeVenter did and say, "All to Jesus I surrender"? Jesus surrendered all for you!

**The Ark of the Covenant
and
The Mercy Seat**

And they shall make an ark of acacia wood: two cubits and a half shall be the length thereof, and a cubit and a half the breadth thereof, and a cubit and a half the height thereof. And thou shalt overlay it with pure gold, within and without shalt thou overlay it, and shalt make upon it a rim of gold round about. And thou shalt cast four rings of gold for it, and put them in the four corners thereof; and two rings shall be in the one side of it, and two rings in the other side of it.

Exodus 25:10–12

CHAPTER 8

The Ark
of the Covenant
(Exodus 25:10–22; 37:1–9)

I n a spirit of reverence, we loose the shoes from our feet, part the veil, and enter the sacred ground of the holy of holies to gaze upon the small golden ark of the covenant. We have the great privilege of viewing the ark and seeing its prophetic fulfill-ment in Christ, a privilege that was unknown to the children of Israel except for two people: Moses, who could approach God at all times before the mercy seat (Ex. 25:22), and the high priest, who could enter once a year to make atonement for his own sins and those of the people. Come, let us enter with boldness, as we have been instructed, and glean the many lessons God has for us.

The Construction of the Ark

The ark was symbolic of God's throne and presence, making it the most sacred article of furniture in the Tabernacle. In fact, the Tabernacle was built to house the ark of the covenant, so that God could dwell among His people. It was the first item of fur-niture made after God instructed Moses to build the Tabernacle (Ex. 25:8–10). It was placed on top of the mercy seat, between the two cherubim, where God's glory dwelt (Ps. 80:1) in the form of a cloud by day and a pillar of fire by night (Ex. 40:34–38).

The ark was called by many names. It was known as "the ark of the testimony" (Ex. 25:22) because it was where the two tablets of the law were kept; "the ark of the covenant" (Num. 10:33), speaking of God's covenant relationship with His people; "the ark of God" (1 Sam. 3:3); "the ark of the Lord GOD" (1 Ki. 2:26); "the holy ark" (2 Chr. 35:3); and "the ark of thy strength" (Ps. 132:8).

The ark was a rectangular chest, three feet nine inches long and two feet three inches wide and high, made of acacia wood and covered with gold inside and out. It had a gold rim encircling its top, gold rings on the four corners, and staves of acacia wood covered with gold to carry it. The lid, called the mercy seat, was of pure gold. On top of the ark, at each end, stood two cherubim of gold facing each other but looking down toward the mercy seat with their wings touching each other as they were stretched out over its top (Ex. 25:10–20).

The ark is one of the clearest types of Jesus Christ presented in the Bible. As with the brazen altar, the table of showbread, and the altar of incense, the acacia wood typifies the Lord's life and ministry. This hard, incorruptible, indestructible wood, which grows in the Sinai Desert, beautifully portrays the humanity of Christ, who came from "a root out of a dry ground" (Isa. 53:2) and was absolutely sinless in His birth (Lk. 1:35) and life (1 Pet. 1:19; 2:22). Even His enemies recognized that He was sinless (e.g., Judas, Mt. 27:3–4; Pilate, Lk. 23:4, 14; Pilate's wife, Mt. 27:19; Herod, Lk. 23:15; the thief on the cross, Lk. 23:40–41; and the centurion at the crucifixion, Lk. 23:47). The indestructibility of the wood speaks of Christ in His humanity withstanding the fire of crucifixion (Mt. 27:33–50) and the decaying effects of the grave (Ps. 16:10; Acts 2:30–34). The gold in the table is emblematic of Jesus' deity. The Bible explicitly states that Jesus is divine (Jn. 1:1; 10:30–33), ascribing such divine attributes to Him as eternal existence (Rev. 1:8), omnipresence (Mt. 28:20), omniscience (Jn. 2:24–25), and omnipotence (Phil. 3:21).

The ark of wood overlaid with gold typifies the union of Jesus' divine and human natures (Phil. 2:6–11). The Scriptures teach that He had two natures but not two personalities. Christ is the God-Man (2 Cor. 5:19), the express image of God (Heb. 1:3), and the embodiment and expression of His fullness (Col. 1:15–19). The gold gave a glow to the wood in the ark, just as the deity of Christ glorified His humanity during His earthly ministry (Acts 2:22; 10:38).

The ark in the holy of holies was symbolic of the Lord's glory in two ways. First, as the ark dwelt among mankind, so Christ was manifested to mankind during His earthly pilgrimage. Second, as the ark represented the throne of God, where He manifested His glory, so Christ is seated at the right hand of God in all of His glory (Eph. 1:19–23).

The Contents of the Ark

Hebrews 9:4 states that the ark contained three objects: "the golden pot that had manna, and Aaron's rod that budded, and the tables of the covenant." It has been suggested that a contradiction exists in the Scriptures, because 1 Kings 8:9 states that only the tablets of the law were in the ark, but this is not a contradiction. Hebrews 9:4 describes the original contents of the ark, while 1 Kings 8:9 records the contents of the ark at the time of Solomon's Temple. Further study of the ark's contents will show that they are more an expression of who Christ is than what He does.

The Manna

The first item mentioned is the "pot that had manna," which was the food provided by God for the children of Israel during their 40 years of wandering in the wilderness. The word *manna* in Exodus 16:15 is a transliteration of two Hebrew words expressed in English as *What is it?* It is also known by three other names in Scripture: "bread from heaven" (Ex. 16:4); "angel's food" (Ps. 78:25); and "light bread" (Num. 21:5). The manna appeared every morning around the camp when the dew fell on the ground, similar to hoar frost (Ex. 16:14). It looked like a small round coriander seed, was white in color, and tasted like wafers made with honey (Ex. 16:31) or oil (Num. 11:7–8). The leader of each home gathered one omer (2 dry quarts) per person every morning (Ex. 16:16). Only one day's supply was collected, except on the sixth day, when they gathered twice as much for the Sabbath (Ex. 16:22), and there was always just the right amount for each Israelite (Ex. 16:18). If any was left on the ground after the gathering, it melted away in the sun's heat (Ex. 16:21). Aaron was commanded to collect an omer of manna in a golden bowl and place it inside the ark (Ex. 16:33). In giving the manna, God revealed that He was able to meet and sustain the physical and spiritual needs of His people.

The manna foreshadowed Christ and His ministry in many ways. Paul called it "spiritual food" (1 Cor. 10:3) because of its supernatural origin, being "bread from heaven" (Ex. 16:4). The Lord referred to Himself as "the true bread from heaven" (Jn. 6:32). The manna was provided for the Israelites in the wilderness, a place that was not their home (Ex. 16:1). The Lord left His home in heaven to enter the wilderness of the world. He had no building in which to be born (Lk. 2:7) nor a place to call His own (Lk. 9:58), and He was buried in a borrowed tomb (Lk. 23:50–53). The manna was free for the taking, just as God freely gave His Son so that we might have spiritual life (Jn. 3:16; 6:51). The Israelites could glean only enough manna to sustain them for a day (Ex. 16:4). Just as we need physical food to sustain us daily, so Christ is our spiritual food, sustaining us each day (Jn. 6:35). The whiteness of the manna (Ex. 16:31) speaks of Christ's spotless purity (1 Pet. 1:19). The manna was ground and baked, picturing Christ's suffering on our behalf (Jn. 6:48–51). The manna was laid in the ark (Ex. 16:33), picturing the Lord before the throne of God on our behalf (Heb. 9:23–24). The resurrected Lord announced to the church at Pergamum that He has "hidden manna" to give to all those who overcome (Rev. 2:17). One day we will feast on the hidden glories of the resurrected Lord in a fuller way. Christ is the true manna and is sufficient to meet the needs of all people (Phil. 4:19), satisfy hungry souls (Mt. 5:6), strengthen believers for service (Phil 4:13), and sustain them in that service (1 Cor. 10:13).

Aaron's Rod that Budded

The second item in the ark was Aaron's rod that budded. The story of the budding rod is recorded in Numbers 16 and 17. Korah, Dathan, and Abiram had gathered 250 leaders from the 12 tribes to challenge Moses and Aaron's right to lead the people. Moses accepted the challenge, and God vindicated his leadership by opening the ground, which swallowed up Korah and all those who stood with him (Num. 16:32). The 250 who had rebelled against Moses' leadership were destroyed by fire from God out of heaven (Num. 16:35).

The next day the congregation of Israel accused Moses of killing the people of God. To provide further proof of Aaron's right to be high priest, God instructed Moses to select a representative from each tribe to bring an almond rod with the name of the tribe engraved on it (Aaron's name was on the rod of the tribe of Levi). The rod of the man God had chosen to be high priest would blossom. All 12 rods were put in the Tabernacle before the testimony. The next morning, Aaron's rod had budded, blossomed, and yielded almonds (17:8). Aaron's rod was placed in the ark for a sign against the rebels, proving that he alone had the right to be high priest.

The budding rod was a picture of Christ's resurrection. Three days after His crucifixion, He broke the bars of death and was mightily resurrected from the grave (Mt. 28:1–9). He validated His resurrection by appearing ten times over a 40-day period. He alone is "the resurrection and the life" (Jn. 11:25).

Not only did Aaron's rod blossom, but it bore fruit (almonds). The Scriptures teach that Christ is the first fruits from the dead (1 Cor. 15:23). Christ was resurrected first, and all true believers will be resurrected at His coming (1 Th. 4:13–18).

Christ also wants to reproduce fruit in us. But if we expect to produce fruit, we must abide as branches in Him, the vine, for without Him we can do nothing (Jn. 15:5). The fruit that He produces in us takes three forms. First, character emerges as we appropriate the fruit of the Spirit (Gal. 5:22–23). Second, as we walk with Him, the fruit of our conduct brings glory to His name (Eph. 4:17–32). Third, converts are the fruit of our witness (Rom. 1:13–15).

The Tablets of the Law

Also in the ark were the tablets of the law. God engraved the moral law (Ex. 20:1–17) on the stones that Moses had hewn. Although they were broken by Moses (Ex. 32:19), a second set was made and put into the ark (Dt. 10:2).

The book of the law that Moses wrote was to be placed "in the side" (lit., by the side) of the ark of the covenant as a witness against the children of Israel (Dt. 31:25–26). Talmudic scholars state that the book of the law was placed in the ark (Baba Bathra, 14), but the Targum of Jonathan states that it was put in a box at the right side of the ark. The last view seems closer to the truth.

Christ's life and ministry were in definite fulfillment of the law. He was "made under the law" (Gal. 4:4). He had the law written within His heart, thus fulfilling the letter of it (Ps. 40:8; Heb. 10:7–9). He did not come to destroy the law but to fulfill it (Mt. 5:17). He bore the curse of the law by being made a curse for us (Gal. 3:13). Paul put it succinctly when he wrote, "For Christ is the end of the law for righteousness to everyone that believeth" (Rom. 10:4).

The Career of the Ark
The Ark Carried before Israel

The ark had a long and illustrious history. It was carried by the Kohathites (Num. 3:30) before the children of Israel to seek a resting place for them as they journeyed from Sinai to Kadesh-barnea (Num. 10:33). Placing the ark before the Israelites pictures the Lord going before us. John wrote, "And when he putteth forth his own sheep, he goeth before them" (Jn. 10:4). Jesus leads us in the way we should go during our pilgrimage on earth.

The ark, borne on the shoulders of the priests, led the way across the Jordan River as the Israelites entered the promised land. At Joshua's command, the priests entered the waters, which parted on both sides, allowing them to go across on dry ground (Josh. 3). This pictures the Lord enabling us to go through the waters of difficulty associated with His will. Remember the words of Paul: "I can do all things through Christ, who strengtheneth me" (Phil. 4:13).

The ark led the way as the Israelites marched around the walls of Jericho for seven days (Josh. 6:4–20), picturing the Lord as He goes before us to fight the battles we face as we walk by faith. God has assured us that we are more than conquerors; we can be triumphant in Christ as we overcome the world through a walk of faith (1 Jn. 5:4).

The Ark's Counsel to Israel

The tribe of Benjamin sinned greatly before God (Jud. 19), and the other tribes decided to war against the Benjamites to punish them (Jud. 20:18–48). Although the other tribes were much stronger militarily, they were defeated in the first two battles and suffered great losses. Then Phineas the priest stood before the ark and sought the Lord's counsel whether to go to battle against the Benjamites a third time. The Lord counseled them to go up to battle, and, in so doing, they defeated the Benjamites. We too must know the mind of Christ to fight the battles confronting us daily.

The Ark Captured From Israel

God allowed the ark to be delivered to the Philistines because of Israel's apostasy. When he heard that the ark had been captured, Eli, the high priest, fell off his seat and died from a broken neck (1 Sam. 4:18). When his daughter-in-law, who was giving birth at the time, heard that the ark had been captured, she stated, "The glory is departed from Israel; for the ark of God is taken" (1 Sam. 4:22). This episode presents another type of Christ as He was delivered into the hands of Gentiles, which eventually resulted in His death (Lk. 18:32–33).

The ark became a curse to the Philistines (1 Sam. 5—6). It was set in the house of Dagon, their vegetation god. The idol fell before the ark twice, the second fall breaking off its head and palms. At the same time, tumors (boils) broke out on the Philistines (1 Sam. 5:9), and the land was overrun with mice (1 Sam. 6:5). The plague on the Philistines did not cease until the ark was returned to Israel (1 Sam. 6:8–12). This is a picture of how Christ will destroy the gods of this world (2 Th. 2:8–9), bring judgment on those who have not worshiped the true and living God (Mt. 25:31–41), and rule in absolute sovereignty over all the earth (Phil 2:9–11; Rev. 11:15).

The Ark Taken by Cart to the Israelites

The men of Kiriath-jearim reclaimed the ark and placed it in the house of Abinadab, where it remained for 20 years (1 Sam. 7:1–2). After David established his throne in Jerusalem, he placed the ark on an ox-drawn cart, in disobedience to God

(Ex. 25:14–15; Num. 3:30–31; 4:15) to transport it to Jerusalem (2 Sam. 6). During the journey, the oxen nearly upset the cart, and Uzziah reached out to steady it but died immediately because he had violated God's holiness by touching the ark. Only the Levites were permitted to carry the ark (Num. 4:15).

Fearing the judgment of God, David did not take the ark into Jerusalem but deposited it in the house of Obed-edom (2 Sam. 6:10–11), where it remained for three months, during which time Obed-edom, a Gentile, was greatly blessed. This is a picture of God's grace to Gentiles who put their faith in Him (Acts 15:14).

Three months later David had the priests carry the ark to Jerusalem, where it was placed in a properly prepared tent (2 Sam. 6:17) until Solomon's Temple was built (2 Chr. 5). The ark dwelling in the midst of Israel is another symbol of Christ, who will tabernacle among His people during the Millennial Kingdom (Rev. 21:3).

The final whereabouts of the ark has been shrouded in speculation since the destruction of Solomon's Temple in 586 B.C. My colleague, Elwood McQuaid, gives a number of interesting views on this subject in his book, *It Is No Dream*. He suggests seven possibilities of what might have happened to the ark. First, it may have been destroyed by the marauding Babylonians who would have been interested in salvaging the gold it contained. It may have been taken back to Babylon as a trophy of war, although it is not among the valuables described in the list of confiscated items in 2 Kings 25.

Second, a rabbinical tradition asserts that it was, at some time, buried by priests under the Temple Mount before the Babylonians captured the city. If this is true, it would still be there, as we know that it has never been unearthed.

Third, another tradition in one of the apocryphal books states that Jeremiah removed the ark from Jerusalem (2 Maccabees 2:4–5). This account says that the location of the cave was lost and awaits disclosure by the Lord at some later date.

Fourth, others believe that the ark was transported to heaven, where it now rests. Support for this view is claimed from

Revelation 11:19. The question is whether this is the actual ark known to Israel or a heavenly version in the celestial Temple.

Fifth, Dr. Benjamin Mazar, who is in charge of all excavations in Jerusalem, does not believe the ark to be in existence. He feels that if it was not destroyed, it would have long since decayed and disintegrated. This view, however, does not take into account the fact that the wood was encased in gold and contained stone articles. He does concede that were he and his associates to discover the ark, it would have a most dramatic effect on the nation and, for that matter, the world.

Sixth, it is noteworthy that Jeremiah said the ark would not be necessary in the ultimate future of Israel (Jer. 3:16).

Seventh, the description of the Millennial Temple in Ezekiel 40—44 does not mention the ark. In the eternal state there will be no need for the ark of the covenant because the Lord will be tabernacled in our midst (Rev. 21:3) [It Is No Dream, pp. 35–38].

During the days of the Tabernacle, God met with His people over the mercy seat of the ark. Today, Christ is our ark of safety and provides all we need in this life and the life to come. He has entered heaven to appear before the court of God as our legal representative, functioning as our advocate and interceding on our behalf.

Let us draw near with expectation and lift our voices in song:

Ah! whither could we flee for aid,
    When tempted, desolate, dismayed;
Or how the host of hell defeat,
    Had suffering saints no mercy seat?

Ah! there on angel wings we soar,
    And sin and sense molest no more;
And heav'n comes down our souls to greet
    While glory crowns the mercy seat.

And thou shalt make a mercy seat of pure gold: two cubits and a half shall be the length thereof, and a cubit and a half the breadth thereof. And thou shalt make two cherubim of gold, of beaten work shalt thou make them, in the two ends of the mercy seat. And make one cherub on the one end, and the other cherub on the other end: even of the mercy seat shall ye make the cherubim on the two ends thereof. And the cherubim shall stretch forth their wings on high, covering the mercy seat with their wings, and their faces shall look one to another; toward the mercy seat shall the faces of the cherubim be. And thou shalt put the mercy seat above upon the ark; and in the ark thou shalt put the testimony that I shall give thee. And there I will meet with thee, and I will commune with thee from above the mercy seat, from between the two cherubim which are upon the ark of the testimony, of all things which I will give thee in commandment unto the children of Israel.

Exodus 25:17–22

CHAPTER 9

The Mercy Seat
(Exodus 25:17–22; 37:6–9)

T he high priest, having meticulously followed all the required steps for ceremonial cleansing, left the holy place and slowly made his way to the brazen altar to offer the appropriate sacrifices for the day of atonement. Conscious of his holy task, he carried out each prescribed step of his ministry in a spirit of deep, adoring awe and precision.

Aware of the tremendous spiritual significance of the day, the Israelites encompassed the exterior of the Tabernacle as far as the eye could see. With sanctified imagination, we can picture the hush that fell over the congregation as they reflected on their personal sins for which the high priest would make atonement.

The High Priest's Worship Before the Mercy Seat

First, the high priest offered a bullock as a sin offering (Lev. 16:6, 11) for himself and his house before he made an offering for the nation of Israel. Next, he took a censer full of burning coals from the brazen altar, put two handfuls of sweet incense into a golden bowl, and entered the holy of holies. He poured the incense on the coals, which emitted a thick, fragrant, cloudy smoke that filled the chamber. The cloud of smoke twisting upward represented the prayers of God's people, offered as protection, on this holiest of all days.

The high priest returned to the brazen altar, took a basin full of the bullock's blood, and again entered the holy of holies to sprinkle the blood on the mercy seat. Dipping his finger into the basin of blood, he sprinkled the mercy seat seven times (Lev. 16:14). The blood made it possible for God to show mercy to the nation of Israel. Sprinkling the blood seven times spoke of the completed atonement.

The high priest chose two goats of equal color, size, and value from the congregation of Israel (Lev. 16:5). Lots were cast by the high priest to determine which of the two goats was to be slain. We do not know how the lots were chosen during the days of the Tabernacle. Dr. Edersheim, in his book, *The Temple*, gives us a very vivid picture of the procedure during the Lord's day. The high priest put the golden lots in an urn, shook it, and, with both hands, drew out the two lots, putting one on the head of each goat (Lev. 16:8). He then tied a tongue-shaped piece of scarlet cloth to the horn of the goat for *azazel* (KJV, *scapegoat*) and another around the throat of the goat to be slain. The scapegoat was turned facing the people until the high priest, at the proper time, transferred the people's sin to it and led it off into the wilderness (*The Temple*, pp. 311–312).

The high priest then offered the first goat as a sin offering. Its blood was sprinkled several times in the Tabernacle. First, it was sprinkled before the mercy seat in the holy of holies in the same manner as the blood of the bullock (Lev. 16:15). Second, he sprinkled the horns of the altar of incense seven times to cleanse it from the contamination of Israel (Ex. 30:10). Third, he went to the brazen altar and mixed the blood of the bullock and the blood of the goat into one basin. Dipping his finger into the basin of blood, he sprinkled the horns of the brazen altar seven times, cleansing it from the uncleanness of Israel (Lev. 16:19).

The congregation of Israel patiently and prayerfully waited outside of the Tabernacle for the high priest to appear before them. Naturally, many questions passed through their minds: Would God accept the blood offered by the high priest? If God did not accept the blood offering, would He slay the high priest in the holy of holies? Would God be merciful to Israel or would He bring judgment? But then the high priest parted the gate of the Tabernacle court with his hands raised toward the people, symbolizing that God had accepted their sacrifice. Joyous praise echoed throughout the congregation—it was like life from the dead! The atonement had been accepted!

Moving quickly, the high priest placed his blood-soaked hands on the head of the scapegoat, transferring the sins of Israel to the goat as he confessed every possible transgression that had been committed in the past year. The scapegoat was then led away into the wilderness, signifying that the sins of Israel, which God had forgiven, were carried away (Lev. 16:20–22).

During the time of the Lord, a priest led the sin-burdened goat out through Solomon's Porch and, according to tradition, through the East Gate, which led directly to the Mount of Olives. Another priest then led the scapegoat away into the wilderness for a distance of about 12 miles. The distance was divided into ten stations, each station extending half a Sabbath's day journey, in order for the priest to rest during his journey. When the priest arrived at the designated spot, he took the scarlet cloth from the goat's horn, tore it in half, placed one piece back on the goat's horn, and took the other piece back to Jerusalem. The goat, bearing the sins of Israel, was then pushed backward to its death over a designated precipice. After Jesus' arrest, the chief priest and elders turned Him over to the Gentile governor, Pontius Pilate (Mt. 27:1–2), who allowed Him to be crucified to bear the sins of the people.

According to Jewish tradition, when the sacrifice was fully accepted, the scarlet cloth tied to the scapegoat's horn became white, symbolizing God's gracious promise in Isaiah 1:18: "though your sins be as scarlet, they shall be as white as snow;

though they be red like crimson, they shall be as wool." But Dr. Edersheim states that, according to tradition, this miracle did not take place during the 40 years preceding the destruction of the Temple (*The Temple*, p. 312). Interestingly, it stopped around the time that the Lord was crucified.

The word translated "scapegoat" (Lev. 16:8, 10, 26) is *azazel* in Hebrew and denotes the idea of an *entire removal*; thus, the scapegoat completely removed the sins of Israel. Although the sins of the people were removed, they were not taken away and destroyed until Christ came. The writer to the Hebrews stated, "For it is not possible that the blood of bulls and of goats should take away sins" (Heb. 10:4). Christ fulfilled the requirements of the sin offering by taking the sins of the world on Himself: "For he hath made him, who knew no sin, to be sin for us, that we might be made the righteousness of God in him" (2 Cor. 5:21; cp. 1 Pet. 2:24). It was only through the shed blood of the Lord Jesus that our sins were completely blotted out. The writer to the Hebrews clearly stated, "Neither by the blood of goats and calves, but by his own blood he entered in once into the holy place, having obtained eternal redemption for us" (Heb. 9:12). And again, "But now once, in the end of the ages, hath he appeared to put away sin by the sacrifice of himself" (Heb. 9:26).

Then the high priest went into the holy place, put off his linen garments, washed his body, put on his priestly garments, and went before the brazen altar to offer a burnt offering for himself and the people. At the same time he burned the fat of the bullock and goat from the sin offering on the brazen altar. The skin, flesh, and dung of the sin offering (bullock and goat) were burned outside the camp (Lev. 16:23–27).

Christ is our sin offering, becoming an outcast condemned to endure the suffering and shame of crucifixion, so that He might sanctify us through His own blood by suffering outside the camp of Jerusalem (Heb. 13:11–12). There is a particular exhortation to believers in connection with Christ's suffering. We are expected to share the insults and shame of His cross by living separated lives in the world, suffering, if necessary, for our faith in Him (Heb. 13:13). Before His crucifixion, Jesus said, "Take up [your] cross, and follow me" (Mt. 16:24).

The only duty left for the high priest was to offer the prescribed evening sacrifices (Num. 29:7, 11) before his ministry was concluded on this special day.

The question is often asked, How do the Jewish people atone for sin today, since there is no Temple or priesthood? Modern Judaism teaches that they can receive forgiveness without a Temple, sacrifice, or mediating priest. They reason as follows: Because God allowed the Temple and priesthood to be destroyed, forgiveness is acquired by going directly to God. People are to recite long prayers, repent of every conscious sin, and make reconciliation to all those they have sinned against in the past year. Then God will forgive them of their sins.

Although this seems like a logical way to receive forgiveness of sins, it is not the teaching of the Jewish Scriptures. The Word of God clearly shows that forgiveness of sin can only be obtained by approaching God in the way He has set forth. Leviticus 17:11 says, "for it is the blood that maketh an atonement for the soul." The blood gives significance to the day of atonement. If there is no blood in Judaism to atone for the soul, how are they able to acquire forgiveness on the day of atonement? They cannot! But God has provided a blood atonement for the Jewish people. Paul said, "For there is one God, and one mediator between God and men, the man, Christ Jesus, Who gave himself a ransom for all" (1 Tim. 2:5–6).

Hebrews 9 and 10 clearly state that Jesus the Messiah shed His blood as the one offering necessary to atone for sins (Heb. 9:11–15, 26, 28). Today, the Jewish people have an atonement through the mediating priest, Jesus Christ. He alone can atone for sin.

The Propitiatory Work of the Mercy Seat

In the time of the Tabernacle, the mercy seat was made a place of propitiation when the sacrificial blood was sprinkled on it once a year. The mercy seat, typifying the divine throne of God, was transformed from a throne of judgment to a throne of grace when it was sprinkled with the atoning blood. Today, sinners have a mercy seat in the blood-sprinkled body of Jesus Christ, who died on the cross as an atonement to expiate sin.

The term "mercy seat" in Hebrews 9:5 is a translation of the Greek word *hilasterion*, which means *propitiation*. The word is used in the Septuagint Version (Greek translation of the Old Testament) to refer to the mercy seat (see Lev. 16:14) where the atoning blood was sprinkled. In English, *propitiation* has the idea of *appeasing or placating the anger of a god*, thus buying his love, but this is not the concept found in the New Testament. Because of His love for mankind, God initiated a plan by which people could be reconciled back to Him. John wrote, "Herein is love, not that we loved God, but that he loved us, and sent his Son to be the propitiation for our sins" (1 Jn. 4:10).

In the New Testament, *propitiation* has the idea of *satisfying the righteous demands of a holy God*, making it possible for the removal of sin that stands between God and mankind. This was accomplished by Christ's substitutionary death on the cross for sin. His shed blood completely satisfied all the demands of a holy God for the judgment of sin, thus making it possible for God to declare and treat as righteous all those who come to Him.

The extent of propitiation is universal. John stated, "And he is the propitiation for our sins, and not for ours only, but also for the sins of the whole world" (1 Jn. 2:2). The Lord's propitiatory work is sufficient for everyone but is only efficacious to those who willingly receive it. Today, people do not have to continually beg God to forgive their sins, because God has once and for all been propitiated through Jesus' blood. All people have to do to be reconciled to God is receive the finished work of the Lord Jesus on their behalf. Paul summed it up well when he wrote, "For all have sinned, and come short of the glory of God, Being justified freely by his grace through the redemption that is in Christ Jesus, Whom God hath set forth to be a propitiation through faith in his blood, to declare his righteousness for the remission of sins that are past, through the forbearance of God; To declare, I say, at this time his righteousness, that he might be just, and the justifier of him who believeth in Jesus" (Rom. 3:23–26).

If you have not been reconciled to God, why tarry? Right now, recognize your sinful condition; by faith, come to the mercy seat through the shed blood of Jesus Christ and be declared righteous through His grace.

What a comfort to have a blood-bought mercy seat to which we can retreat from the stormy winds of the world that blow against our Christian walk. Hugh Stowell caught a vision of the sublime privilege we have to come before the mercy seat and find comfort in time of need. In 1828, he penned the words to a hymn that he originally entitled "Peace at the Mercy Seat," but the title was later changed to "From Every Stormy Wind That Blows." Two stanzas of the hymn sum up the fellowship that awaits each blood-bought believer who comes to the mercy seat through Jesus Christ.

> From every stormy wind that blows,
>   From every swelling tide of woes,
> There is a calm, a sure retreat:
>   'Tis found beneath the mercy seat.
>
> There is a place where Jesus sheds
>   The oil of gladness on our heads;
> A place than all besides more sweet:
>   It is the blood-bought mercy seat.

Oh, Christian friends, no longer is the mercy seat open only once a year. No longer do we need an earthly high priest to intercede on our behalf. No longer must sacrifice be slain for us. The veil has been torn away. God bids us come boldly to the throne of grace to obtain mercy and find grace in any time of need. Accept the invitation. Rejoice in the privilege. Come, bask in the glorious presence of the Lord, which is eternally offered and open to you!

PART II
THE SACRIFICIAL SYSTEM

For the life of the flesh is in the blood; and I have given it to you upon the altar to make an atonement for your souls; for it is the blood that maketh an atonement for the soul.

Leviticus 17:11

CHAPTER 10

The Sacrificial Offerings

(Leviticus 17:11)

S ince the dawn of creation, people have sought to worship by offering sacrifices to their deities. Sometimes the sacrifices were from the fruits of their own hands and sometimes they were animals that they had slain (Gen. 4:3–4). From the Moabites in the Middle East to the Aztecs in South America, people have sacrificed to placate the gods they served, hoping that they would produce good crops, prosper throughout the year, enjoy good health, and be victorious over hostile peoples living around them.

The archaeologist's spade has revealed elaborate sacrificial systems developed by ancient Semitic peoples in the Middle East. Such documents as the Ras Shama text, describing the sacrificial customs of the Phoenicians, Canaanites, and Carthaginians, reveal a similarity between them and the Mosaic system practiced by Israel.

Human sacrifice was practiced by those in the Middle East. The Canaanites held a strong belief in the efficacy of sacrificing their firstborn in the wake of impending national or individual disaster, hoping to divert the disaster by placating their god. When the battle went against the king of Moab, he offered his eldest son for a burnt offering on the wall of his city (2 Ki. 3:26–27). King Ahaz did the same thing when he made his son pass through the fire in the valley of Topheth (2 Ki. 16:3; Jer. 7:31), although human sacrifice was not the norm in Israel and was condemned by God.

The Purpose of Sacrifice

Many theories have been suggested in an attempt to explain why people offered sacrifices through the centuries. Some hold to a *gift* theory, which states that sacrifices were offered to obtain favor from the gods; that is, people *gave* to their gods in order to *get* from their gods. Others believe in a *magic* theory, which suggests that sacrifices were originally offered to demons to drive evil spirits out of sinful or sick people and into the sacrificial victims, which were then destroyed. The offerers were trying to placate the will of their gods through magical forces. The *table-bond* theory was a sacrificial meal shared by the offerers and their gods with the view of establishing fellowship and communion. The *communion* theory is a variation of the *table-bond* view and states that both the animals to be sacrificed and the ones sacrificing possessed a divine nature; thus, by eating the animals the offerers "ate the god" and received the strength and power inherent in the divine nature of the animals. Finally, there is the *homage* theory. Sacrifices were offered, not because of a sense of sin, but out of a feeling of dependence upon a deity. By showing homage and obedience to their gods, people gained their favor. When studying the Bible, it becomes apparent that these theories in no way explain the scriptural purpose for people sacrificing to the true God.

The concept of sacrifice was originated in the mind of God and was intended to provide an atonement for sin so that people could approach Him. Sacrifices were to be offered as a vicarious and substitutionary expiation for people's sins, which were symbolically transferred to animals used to make atonement and propitiate the wrath of God against the sinners (Lev 1:1—7:38). This purpose for sacrifices is consistently presented from Genesis to Malachi.

The Sacrifices of the Patriarchs

In the beginning, Adam and Eve enjoyed direct fellowship and communication with God, not needing a sacrifice. But after their fall into sin, it became necessary for God to introduce the sacrificial system as a means by which sinful people could approach Him.

The first biblical allusion to a sacrifice is recorded in Genesis 3:21, where God provided coats of skins to clothe Adam and Eve after their fall. Although the text does not state that God provided atonement for this sins through an animal sacrifice, it must be assumed that He taught them the concept directly or indirectly through this act of sacrifice. Later the Scriptures clearly teach that God can forgive sin only by means of a blood atonement, for how else but from their parents did Cain and Abel know to bring a sacrifice before God in worship?

The first sacrifices mentioned in the Scriptures were offered by Cain and Abel (Gen. 4:3–5). Their circumstances were the same—both were born outside of Eden of sinful parents—but they offered different sacrifices to the Lord. Cain offered from "the fruit of the ground" (Gen. 4:3), and Abel offered "the firstlings of his flock" (Gen. 4:4). God did not accept Cain's sacrifice, and the writer to the Hebrews records the reason: "By faith Abel offered unto God a more excellent sacrifice than Cain, by which he obtained witness that he was righteous, God testifying of his gifts" (Heb. 11:4). Abel's sacrifice was more excellent because it was the prescribed blood offering required by God, which Cain failed to bring.

Some may say that we are reading too much into the text, since God does not specifically say that Cain's sacrifice was rejected because it was bloodless, but God taught Adam and Eve the necessity of a blood atonement when He slew the animals in

Eden to cover their nakedness. From Abel onward, people offered blood sacrifices when worshiping God.

Immediately upon leaving the ark, Noah offered a burnt offering to the Lord of every clean beast and fowl (Gen. 8:20). Noah did this in appreciation to God for his survival through the flood. The Lord's acceptance of Noah's burnt offering is evidenced by the fact that He smelled the soothing aroma (lit., smell of satisfaction) of the sacrifice and promised to never again curse the earth by flood (Gen. 8:21–22; 9:15). The covenant God made with Noah centered around a blood sacrifice.

The patriarch Job offered sacrifices on behalf of his children (Job 1:5) and three friends (Job 42:7–9) to atone for their sins and sanctify them before God.

During his journey through Canaan, Abraham built altars to commemorate the times when the Lord appeared to him (Gen. 12:7–8; 13:4, 18). Although the text says only that Abraham "called upon the name of the LORD" (Gen. 12:8), not mentioning a sacrifice, it can be assumed that sacrifices were included. Why else would he have built altars?

The first mention of a sacrifice by Abraham was in connection with the covenant that God made with him (Gen. 15:7–21). The animals Abraham sacrificed were the very ones stipulated later in the Mosaic law. It was customary in Abraham's day for two men who made a covenant to walk between the bleeding parts of the sacrifice (Jer. 34:18–19). When God made the covenant with Abraham, He passed between the two halves of the animals, in the form of a flaming firepot and burning lamp, while Abraham passively slept. This was symbolic of the unconditional covenant that God made with Abraham, whereby God assured Abraham that He would perform all the provisions of the covenant—it was not based on the faithfulness of Abraham but on the faithfulness of Abraham's God.

The sacrifices offered by Isaac and Jacob followed the same pattern as Abraham's. After the Lord appeared to Isaac at Beersheba to confirm the Abrahamic Covenant with him, Isaac built an altar and called upon the Lord (Gen. 26:23–25), as did his father. Jacob did the same thing at Bethel when God confirmed the Abrahamic Covenant with him (Gen. 28:13–17). He also offered a sacrifice to seal the covenant between himself and Laban (Gen. 31:54). Jacob stopped at Beersheba to offer a sacrifice before migrating to Egypt (Gen. 46:1–7).

During the 400 years that Israel dwelt in Egypt, there is no record that they built altars or made sacrifices. Up to this point, it seems that the patriarchs offered sacrifices only in places where God manifested Himself to them. The next recorded sacrifice by Israel was on the eve of Passover, when each household killed the Passover lamb (Ex. 12:6).

The Prescribed Sacrifices

In Moses' confrontation with Pharaoh, his continual request was "let us go . . . three days' journey into the wilderness, that we may sacrifice to the LORD our God" (Ex. 3:18; cp. 5:1–3; 8:25–28; 10:24–26). Sacrifices were initially introduced to the nation of Israel as an atonement for their sins, a substitute for Israel's firstborn, resulting in their redemption.

On the tenth day of Nisan (March–April), each family selected a Passover yearling lamb, without blemish, to be slain at twilight on the 14th day of the month (Ex. 12:1–6). The lamb's blood, sprinkled on the doorposts of the house, became a substitutionary atonement for all the occupants of the house (Ex. 12:12–13). The Israelites were to keep God's ordinance of the Passover throughout their generations as a memorial of this great deliverance (Ex. 12:14). The Passover lamb's being slain and its blood sprinkled on the doorposts as an atonement pictured Christ who, as the paschal lamb, would make atonement to take away sin (Jn. 1:29; 1 Cor. 5:7; 1 Pet. 1:18–20).

After their deliverance from Egypt, the Israelites traveled to Mount Sinai, where God entered into a covenant relationship with them. The Mosaic Covenant, as it is called, was sealed with a sacrifice offered by Moses. He built an altar at the foot of the mount consisting of 12 pillars representing the 12 tribes of Israel. Young men (not priests) sacrificed a burnt offering and a peace offering to the Lord, and the blood of the sacrifice was distributed, half put in a basin and half sprinkled on the altar. The covenant was read, accepted by Israel, and consummated by God and Israel through the sprinkling of blood on both the people and the written covenant (Ex. 19:5–8).

The burnt offering atoned for the people's sins and was symbolic of their unconditional surrender to God, bringing them into a covenant relationship with Him. The peace offering, on the other hand, was symbolic of the reconciliation and fellowship that the Israelites were to experience within the covenant. The blood was not sprinkled on the people until it had been presented and accepted on the altar. The blood applied to the people formally cleansed them from sin and consecrated them to God's service. Through the sprinkling of the sacrificial blood and by their voluntary acceptance of being obedient to the covenant provisions, Israel officially became the people of God.

A number of lessons can be seen in Israel's covenant relationship with God. First, Israel had to atone for their sins before entering into the covenant with God. Second, the covenant, although legal and binding, was entered into by God through an act of pure grace, meaning that the covenant embodied grace as well as law. Third, God promised to deal graciously with the Israelites if they endeavored to follow Him in obedience, even though there were times when they would disobey Him. The Tabernacle was revealed to Moses as the place where Israel could come before God in sacrificial worship. Later the Temple was built on Mount Moriah in Jerusalem and became the place of sacrifice for Israel.

The altar in both the Tabernacle and the Temple was the focal point of the sacrifice. The Hebrew word for *altar* is *mizbeach*, which comes from the word *zavach*, meaning a *place of slaughter*. Not only was it a place of slaughter but a place where the atoning blood from the sacrifices was sprinkled.

The Tabernacle and Temple, with the altar of sacrifice, were provided so that sinful people could approach God, for the law clearly taught, "it is the blood that maketh an atonement for the soul" (Lev.

17:11). The meaning of the verse is that the blood makes atonement by means of the soul; that is, by means of the life that it contains. Because blood represents the animal's life and is the means by which it is kept alive, it also serves to make atonement for the soul of the one sacrificing. Thus, the animal's life is presented as a substitute for the life of the one offering the sacrifice.

The Five Sacrificial Offerings

In the first seven chapters of Leviticus, God set forth the principles and restrictions under which Israel was to sacrifice. Every detail of the sacrifices and their implementation was revealed by the Lord.

The five Levitical offerings were not only meaningful to the Israelites but have a prophetic fulfillment in some aspect of the suffering and death of Christ. In the burnt offering (Lev. 1), a whole animal was consumed on the altar, signifying the complete and voluntary consecration of the Israelites. It typified Christ's voluntarily surrender to the Father's will when He offered Himself on the cross. The meal offering (Lev. 2) was an expression of the Israelites' thanksgiving and recognition of God's sovereignty over them. It typified Christ's perfect obedience to God the Father, which revealed His perfect character and His suffering on behalf of sinful mankind. The peace offering (Lev. 3) spoke of the Israelites experiencing peace and fellowship with God. It typified Christ as the believers' peace, having reconciled them back to God so they can enjoy peace and fellowship with Him. The sin offering (Lev. 4) was brought by the Israelites as a substitute to make atonement for their sins. It typified Christ becoming sin for mankind, dying in their place to take away their sins. The trespass offering (Lev. 5) differed from the sin offering. In the sin offering, people offered for themselves as sinners, but in the trespass offering, they sacrificed for acts of sin they had committed. The sin offering atoned for the guilt of sinners, whereas in the trespass offering, sacrifice was made to offer satisfaction and reparation for wrongs committed against God and their fellowmen. It typified Christ being offered on the cross for the transgressions of others and rendering the fullest satisfaction to God for the wrongs and injuries done to Him by mankind.

The five offerings were divided into sweet and non-sweet offerings. The sweet offerings (burnt, meal, and peace) were so designated because they were acceptable and well pleasing to God, not being offered in respect to the sin and trespass offerings. Paul spoke of Christ's sacrificial work as a "sweet-smelling savor" (Eph. 5:2), referring to His voluntary obedience to the will of the Father and His death on the cross ascending as a sweet aroma before God.

The two non-sweet offerings were so identified because they dealt with mankind's sin and the shame connected with it. They typify Christ bearing the sin and shame of mankind on the cross.

The Five Sacrifices Offered

Five animals were used in sacrificing, and they portrayed the work of Christ during His earthly ministry. The ox typified Christ as a strong, enduring servant who was obedient unto death (Phil. 2:5–8; Heb. 12:3). The lamb was symbolic of Christ's meekness (Mt. 11:29), purity (1 Pet. 1:19), and silent, voluntary surrender to death on the cross (Isa. 53:7; Acts 8:32–33). The goat referred to sinners separated for judgment (Mt. 25:33), but it also typified Christ, who was numbered with the transgressors (Isa. 53:12; Lk. 23:33; 2 Cor. 5:21; Gal. 3:13). The turtledove and pigeon were symbols of mourning, innocence (Isa. 38:14; 59:11), and poverty (Lev. 5:7). They typified Christ who mourned over the sin of mankind (Lk. 19:41), was innocent (Heb. 7:26), became poor for mankind (Mt. 8:20) but enabled believers to become rich in Him (2 Cor. 8:9), and became the poor people's sacrifice (Lk. 2:24).

The sacrificial system of the Old Testament was only "a shadow of good things to come" (Heb. 10:1) and could never take away sins (Heb. 10:4). The blood of animals had no power to provide redemption. The ritual slayings could only purify the flesh—provide ceremonial cleansing (Heb. 9:13).

But God demanded that such an elaborate sacrificial system be established for a number of reasons. First, by offering a blood sacrifice, people acknowledged that atonement must be made before God for sins. Second, they admitted that another must make substitutionary atonement for them; thus, they could not atone for their own sins. Third, the blood atonement that they offered covered their sins before God, making it possible for Him to withhold judgment. Fourth, it made possible the communion of sinful people with a holy God. Fifth, their sacrifices pointed to the day when Christ would once and for all atone for sin (Heb. 9:26–28).

If his offering be a burnt sacrifice of the herd, let him offer a male without blemish: he shall offer it of his own voluntary will at the door of the tabernacle of the congregation before the Lord. And he shall put his hand upon the head of the burnt offering, and it shall be accepted for him to make atonement for him. And he shall kill the bullock before the Lord: and the priests, Aaron's sons, shall bring the blood, and sprinkle the blood round about upon the altar that is by the door of the tabernacle of the congregation.

Leviticus 1:3–5

CHAPTER 11

The Burnt Offering
(Leviticus 1; 6:8–13)

The sacrificial worship of Israel is detailed in the first seven chapters of Leviticus. Every step was minutely revealed to Moses concerning the five offerings, from the animals to be offered to the duties of the priests who functioned as mediators between God and Israel. From sunup to sundown, every day of the year, thousands of animals were paraded before the priests, killed, and their blood sprinkled on the altar.

There is no significance to the order in which the offerings appear in Leviticus. The first offering listed, the burnt offering, should follow the sin offering, but a number of reasons have been presented for the burnt offering being given first. It was the first offering mentioned in Scripture (Gen. 8:20) and was the offering most frequently presented by the patriarchs long before the Mosaic law stipulated the specific sacrifices to be offered. Most likely the burnt offering encompassed the sin offering in the patriarchal period. The Lord instructed Abraham to offer Isaac as a burnt offering (Gen. 22:2); it was the offering Moses performed in the desert after leaving Egypt (Ex. 5:3); both Jethro

(Ex. 18:12) and Job (Job 1:5) offered it long before the giving of the law at Sinai. It was continually offered as a perpetual sacrifice, night and day, on major feast days, and at new moons in Israel. The term *burnt sacrifice* (v. 3) comes from the Hebrew word *olah*, meaning to *ascend upwards*, and refers to the whole offering that was consumed on the altar and ascended to God. Finally, since the whole sacrifice was consumed on the altar, it represented the fullest form of Israel's consecration and worship.

The Offerings

One of five animals could be selected for the burnt offering. The first three were bulls (v. 2), male sheep, or male goats (v. 10). The burnt offering demanded a male rather than a female animal, although there was no such stipulation made during the patriarchal period. In fact, during the confirmation of the Abrahamic Covenant, a heifer was chosen for the burnt offering (Gen. 15:9). Most likely the male animal was chosen under the law because its strength and horns were symbols of power, picturing Christ, who was selected from the flock of His people and crucified in the strength of His youth as a perfect sacrifice, making reconciliation for the sins of the people (Heb. 2:17).

The fourth and fifth offerings were turtledoves or young pigeons (v. 14). These were poor people's offerings (Lev. 12:8). Mary and Joseph's poverty was evident when they offered birds for a sacrifice at Jesus' dedication (Lk. 2:21–24). These birds were probably chosen because of their abundance and easy acquisition in the land of Israel. There was no sex distinction in the birds, like that of the animals. It was mandatory that two birds be offered, one for a burnt offering and the other for a sin offering (Lev. 5:7; 12:8; 14:22).

Nowhere in the sacrificial system was a hen or a rooster ever used as a sacrifice, yet an old Orthodox Jewish custom prescribed that a hen or rooster be killed on Yom Kippur (the day of atonement) because there was no Temple in which to sacrifice. The bird would be held by the legs and swung over a person's head nine times as the person read, "This instead of me, this is an offering on my account, this is an expiation for me; this rooster, or hen, shall go to his, or her, death . . . and may I enter a long and healthy life" (Hayyim Schuass, *Guide to Jewish Holy Days*, p. 150).

Only clean, domesticated animals, as stipulated in the law, could be used as sacrifices. The docile animals pictorially represented Christ in His first advent, "meek and lowly in heart" (Mt. 11:29).

The type of animals offered by the Israelites were in accordance with what they could afford. Rich people brought bulls; the middle class brought sheep or goats; and the poor brought turtledoves or pigeons. If a rich person brought a poor person's offering, God was robbed of His rightful due. Often the priests would not accept a sacrifice if it was beneath what the person could afford.

God wants believers to give their best, whether it is talent or treasure. If the wealthy give meager offerings when they have great possessions, they are robbing God. Often Christians bring gifts of no value to the church. God does not want us to offer that which costs us nothing, as many did in Israel (Mal. 1:7–8, 13). Believers are to give according to the way God has prospered them (1 Cor. 16:1–2) and in a cheerful manner (2 Cor. 9:7).

The Offerers

The Sanctuary

The Israelites personally, of their own voluntary will, presented their offerings at the door of the tabernacle (v. 3). Gazing into the Tabernacle court, the offerers could see the bloodstained brazen altar from which their burnt offerings would ascend to God. They must have been impressed with the meaning of the sacrifice—God could be approached only through the shedding of blood. The same is true with believers today. They must voluntarily come through Jesus, who is the only door into the presence of God (Jn. 10:7–9; 14:6).

The word *offering* (Heb., *qorban*) means something that is *brought near* to the altar and speaks of the sacrificial gifts that were voluntarily presented. By presenting their sacrifices, the offerers were acknowledging a number of things: They believed in the true and living God; they believed God had to be approached properly in worship according to the pattern given by Moses; they desired to follow the Lord in complete consecration through obedience to His will. The same is true for believers today; they are instructed to voluntarily offer their lives to the Lord in service.

The voluntary nature of the burnt offering speaks of Christ's willingness to leave the glories of heaven, be born and live in humility as a man, and freely give Himself to die on the cross for the sins of the world (Phil. 2:5–8; Heb. 10:5–7).

The Substitute

When the Israelites pressed their hands on the heads of the burnt offerings (v. 4), a meaningful identification took place. The offerers identified with the sacrifices as their substitutes—the animals were substituting their lives for those of the Israelites. A double identification took place: The sinful lives of the Israelites were committed to the animals, and the acceptability of the offerings were transmitted to the Israelites. The shed blood of the animals symbolically represented the offerers' lives freely surrendered. Thus, the sacrifices were accepted by God as an atonement (v. 4) for the offerers, protecting them from divine wrath.

Although it is not stated that the offerers confessed their sins during the presentation of burnt offerings, it is implied by laying hands on the animals to be sacrificed. This is a graphic illustration of what occurred on the day of atonement when the high priest laid his hands on the live goat and confessed Israel's sins over it (Lev. 16:21–22). The priest led the sin-burdened goat out through Solomon's Porch and the East Gate, which led directly to the Mount of Olives. At the top of the mount, a Gentile led the goat into the wilderness of Judea and freed it, signifying that the sins of Israel, which had been forgiven by God, were carried away (Lev. 16:20–22).

The identification with the sacrificial animal is a picture of the Christians' identification with Christ (Rom. 4:5; 6:3–11) who died in their place (2 Cor. 5:21).

The Slaying

The Israelites killed the bullocks, sheep, or goats on the north side of the brazen altar (v. 11). When they drew the sharp knives across the animals' throats, killing them, their responsibility was fulfilled concerning the burnt offering. This act left an indelible impression on their minds concerning the significance of the sacrifice. They realized that innocent animals were suffering the death that they deserved. It presented an unforgettable picture of the horror of sin and the price that had to be paid to atone for it. The meaning of commitment lingered in their minds; every time they saw a bull, sheep, or goat, this act of commitment would be brought to remembrance.

Today, the Holy Spirit, through the Word of God, impresses on believers the meaning of Christ's vicarious death on their behalf. Like the Israelites who killed the offerings, believers must remember that in their unregenerated state, it was their sins that crucified Christ (Acts 4:27).

The Officiating Priests

The Mosaic law detailed the specific functions required of the priests for each sacrifice. First, they caught the blood that gushed from the slain animals and sprinkled it "round about upon the altar" (v. 5), making it possible for God to show mercy to the ones offering the sacrifices.

The priests functioned as mediators between God and the people when they sprinkled the blood on the altar. Likewise Christ, who is the believers' mediating high priest, offered His own blood once to put away sin (Heb. 9:11–15; 10:26).

The priests taking the sacrifices from the Israelites presented a picture of Christ giving Himself over to the Father's will. During His agonizing time in the Garden of Gethsemane, Jesus prayed, "O my Father, if it be possible, let this cup pass from me; nevertheless, not as I will, but as thou wilt"(Mt. 26:39). While hanging on the cross, He committed His destiny into the hands of the Father (Lk. 23:46).

The second step for the priests was to flay the animals (v. 6). The skin went to them (Lev. 7:8), but the remainder of the animals was offered to God. The sacrifices were meticulously divided into the proper pieces, and each piece was examined for signs of blemish or disease.

An offering of fowl was handled somewhat differently. The offerers were not required to lay hands on the heads of the birds, nor were they to kill them; that was the priests' ministry (vv. 14–15). The birds were killed by wringing off their heads, and the blood was then wrung out at the side of the altar (v. 15) for an atonement. The birds' crops and feathers were removed and cast on the ash heap near the east side of the altar (v. 16). The birds were not divided like the animals, but were cut down the center, spreading them open (v. 17), and the insides were removed.

The third step was to prepare the altar by putting fire and wood on it (v. 7), indicating that more fuel was added for each new sacrifice. Once the fire on the altar was initially kindled, it was kept burning perpetually by the priests (Lev. 6:13). Fire mentioned in connection with the altar speaks of God's holiness (Heb. 12:29) and judgment (Lev. 10:1–2). Fire mentioned in connection with the sacrifices on the altar symbolizes God's judgment on the animals for the sake of the offerers. The perpetual fire on the altar is typical of two truths. First, God's standards for holiness and justice are unchangeable. Second, by means of the altar, God was always ready to receive the Israelites' sacrificial worship whenever they presented it.

The fourth step was to wash the organs and legs of the animals (v. 9) before placing the pieces on the altar, because these parts were subject to defilement. This act symbolized the inward and outward cleansing of the sacrifices to be offered and presented a two-fold picture of the inward and outward walk of Christ and Christians. Christ was the perfect sacrifice, "Who did no sin, neither was guile found in his mouth" (1 Pet. 2:22). Christians must be cleansed inwardly for service by "the washing of water by the word" (Eph. 5:26), which will manifest itself outwardly in a holy walk. In washing the disciples' feet, Jesus symbolized the need for daily cleansing in order to have unbroken fellowship with God (Jn. 13:1–17).

The fifth step for the priests was to offer the washed pieces, in the same order in which they appeared in the animals' bodies, on the altar (v. 8). The burnt sacrifices then ascended in a smoky vapor as "a sweet savor unto the LORD" (v. 9). The burnt, meal, and peace offerings were all called "sweet savor" because they were not offered for sin. *Sweet savor* means that the offering *pleased God*. Paul spoke of Christ's sacrificial work as "a sweet-smelling savor" (Eph. 5:2), referring to His voluntary obedience to the will of the Father and His death on the cross ascending as a sweet aroma before God. The lives and testimonies of Christians are a sweet savor to the Lord as well (2 Cor. 2:15–16).

The final step for the priests, after completing the sacrifices, was to set aside their priestly garments, put on linen attire (Lev. 6:10), carry the ashes outside of the camp, and put them in a clean place (Lev. 6:11). Disposing of the remains pictured Christ's burial. After His sacrifice had been completed, He was taken from the cross by Joseph of Arimathaea, wrapped in clean linen cloth, and laid in a new tomb (Mt. 27:57–60).

The message of the burnt offering is complete consecration. It is a type of the Lord's complete consecration to the Father's will by giving Himself totally for the sins of mankind. Christ's consecration can be seen through His birth (Heb. 10:5–7), walk (Jn. 8:29), agony in the garden (Mt. 26:39), and death (Phil. 2:8). The Father's testimony to His consecration was summed up by Peter: "For he received from God, the Father, honor and glory, when there came such a voice to him from the excellent glory, This is my beloved Son, in whom I am well pleased" (2 Pet. 1:17).

Christians are obligated to completely consecrate themselves to the Lord. They are to count themselves as "dead indeed unto sin, but alive unto God through Jesus Christ, our Lord" (Rom. 6:11). They are to present their bodies as living and holy sacrifices that will be accepted by God (Rom. 12:1). The burnt offering was to be offered daily by the priests (Lev. 6:12) as a continual reminder to the Israelites of their consecration to God. Likewise, believers must yield their lives in daily consecration to the Lord if they are to have a meaningful and effective spiritual walk.

And when any will offer a meal offering unto the Lord, his offering shall be of fine flour, and he shall pour oil upon it, and put frankincense thereon; And he shall bring it to Aaron's sons, the priests: and he shall take thereout his handful of the flour thereof, and of the oil thereof, with all the frankincense thereof: and the priest shall burn the memorial of it upon the altar, to be an offering made by fire, of a sweet savor unto the Lord. And the remnant of the meal offering shall be Aaron's and his sons': it is a thing most holy of the offerings of the Lord made by fire.

Leviticus 2:1–3

CHAPTER 12

The Meal Offering
(Leviticus 2; 6:14–23)

When the term *Levitical offering* is mentioned, the thought of blood sacrifices flashes across the minds of most people. While it is true that the offerings in the Levitical system were blood sacrifices, there was one exception. The meal offering was a bloodless offering, consisting of grain presented to the Lord.

The Hebrew word *meal* (*minchah*) means *gift* and refers to any gift presented to God (Gen. 4:3) or mankind (Gen. 32:13). In this passage of Scripture, it refers to the Israelites presenting their meal offerings in thanksgiving for God's love and goodness bestowed on them.

The Offerings

The meal offering could be presented in one of three forms, the first being uncooked flour (vv. 1–2). Unlike the blood sacrifices, labor went into the preparation of the meal offerings. The meal had to be crushed, ground, and sifted 13 times to become fine flour (v. 1), picturing Christ's ministry. Fine flour speaks of the evenness and uniformity of the Lord's character and service. He was scourged and crucified for the sins of mankind. During His earthly ministry, Jesus went through the sifting process of Satan's temptation and the religious leaders' testing, yet no sin was found in Him.

The uncooked flour pictures the labor of the Israelites. They had to plant, water, weed, harvest, crush, grind, and sift the grain before offering it to the Lord. For the labors of Christians to be accepted and blessed by the Lord, they must be presented with pure motives, in love, and in the power of the Holy Spirit.

The second form of meal offering was unleavened cakes (v. 4), which could be prepared in one of three ways: kneading the flour into unleavened cakes and baking it in the oven (v. 4), picturing the unseen suffering of the Lord at the hand of God the Father (Mt. 27:45–46); baking the cakes in a pan (griddle) [v. 5], picturing His intense suffering at the hand of Satan (Gen. 3:15); or baking the cakes in a frying pan (v. 7), picturing the visible suffering of Christ at the hand of mankind (Mt. 27:27–31). The meal offering went a step beyond being fine flour, because more preparation was involved. It also pictured believers going a step farther in their service for the Lord.

The third form of meal offering was green ears of grain, dried over fire, and beaten to remove the grain (v. 14). In John 12:24, Jesus pictured Himself as a grain of wheat that had to die to produce fruit. A grain that falls into the ground dies, but through its death the life of the kernel is freed from its encasement and regenerates itself into thousands of other grains possessing the same nature. Through death, Jesus brought resurrection life to all who will put their faith in His finished work on the cross. The grain was scorched, another picture of Jesus going through the fire of suffering to redeem mankind. Beating the grain typified Christ's scourging and beating (Mt. 27:26, 30). The offering was to be of the first fruits (v. 14), a definite type of Christ, who is the first fruits of the resurrection (1 Cor. 15:20, 23) and appears in heaven representing all believers, who one day will be resurrected in their glorified bodies (Phil. 3:20–21; Jas. 1:18).

Various ingredients were added to or omitted from the meal offering. Leaven, which could not be used in the offering (vv. 4, 11), was made by kneading flour (without salt) into a ball and allowing it to stand until it fermented. It was not used at Passover (Ex. 12:8, 15–20), the Feast of Unleavened Bread (Lev. 23:6–8), or in any offering placed on the altar (Ex. 23:18; Lev. 2:11), with two exceptions. Leaven was permitted in the peace offering (Lev. 7:13) and the two wave loaves presented at the time of first fruits (Lev. 23:17).

First, the Israelites presented *unleavened* cakes (Lev. 7:12) with the peace offering, picturing the sinless Christ, who provides peace for believers, reconciling them back to God (Eph. 2:13–18). Second, they offered leavened bread (Lev. 7:13) as a thanksgiving offering for the peace God provided for them. Leavened bread typifies believers making peace with God through the proper sacrifices, although evil still exists in them. In the wave offering (Lev. 23:17), the same picture was presented, but the application was to the church, not to individuals.

In Scripture, leaven always pictures impurity and evil (1 Cor. 5:6–8). Jesus compared the evil doctrines of the Pharisees and the Sadducees (Mt. 16:12) with that of leaven.

Honey could not be used in the meal offering (Lev. 2:11) for a number of reasons. First, honey, like leaven, is a fermenter and corrupter when used in the preparation of vinegar. Second, honey represents natural sweetness, which is pleasant to the taste and something to be desired, but it is a symbol of carnal pleasure. Although very tasty in the mouth, honey becomes sour in the stomach if too much is eaten (Prov. 25:16, 27). Third, honey was offered in the abominable religious practices of the heathenistic people living around the Israelites. These points can be applied to Christ's ministry. He relied not on the natural graces of the sweetness of His person to persuade men, but on the power of the Holy Spirit. Christ also turned away from the sweet things of life—whether they were relationships or material comforts—if they interfered with His mission on earth. There was no element of sweetness in His sacrificial death on the cross; rather, it was cruel suffering.

Olive oil was to be mixed into the meal offerings (vv. 2, 4–5), symbolizing the anointing power of the Holy Spirit, the person of the Godhead who administers the plans, purposes, and programs of God on earth. The Holy Spirit played a major role in the ministry of Christ. He was conceived (Mt. 1:18–20), baptized (Mt. 3:16), anointed (Heb. 1:9), empowered for service (Lk. 4:14, 18), and resurrected (Rom. 8:11) by the Holy Spirit.

The Holy Spirit is operative in believers in many ways. They are born of the Spirit (Jn. 3:3–6), baptized into the body of Christ (1 Cor. 12:12–13), blessed with gifts for service (1 Cor. 12:7–11, 27–30; Eph. 4:11), and empowered to witness for the Lord through the Holy Spirit (Acts 1:8).

Salt was to be used in the meal offering to preserve it from putrefaction and arrest corruption within the meal. Salt was emblematic of God's covenant relationship with Israel; thus, it was called "salt of the covenant of thy God" (v. 13), signifying the enduring covenant relationship between God and Israel, which was never to be broken (cp. Num. 18:19; 2 Chr. 13:5). The meal offering seasoned with salt reminded the Israelites of their covenant relationship with God in several ways: They were to live pure and consistent lives before the Lord; they were to bring their offerings in truthfulness without hypocrisy; they were to be obedient to the commands of God; the covenant signified God's friendship with them and assured that God would be a faithful friend, keeping His promises; and the covenant was eternal, showing them the perpetuity of their relationship with God.

Salt is used in the New Testament as a symbol of the relationship of Christians to God. They are to be "the salt of the earth" (Mt. 5:13). Just as salt arrests corruption, so Christians are to dispel the tide of Satanic corruption manifested in the world. Their speech is to be "seasoned with salt" (Col. 4:6), so that they can "minister grace unto the hearers" (Eph. 4:29); by means of the tongue, the lives of believers are exposed. Salt is not insipid but has tang, as will Christians whose lives are filled with the Holy

Spirit. But salt can lose its savor or taste (Mt. 5:13). Christians are not to lose their savor by allowing sin to dwell in their lives. When believers have lost their savor, they become unusable for God's service and must be set aside. The end result is that they become noneffective in their testimony to the world, and people will trample their witness under foot.

Frankincense was to be sprinkled on the top of the meal offering (vv. 1–2, 15–16). Frankincense should not be confused with the incense burned on the altar of incense, since it was a different substance. Frankincense was made from the fragrant white gum that exudes from the salar tree found in Arabia. It was never to be used for private purposes (Ex. 30:31–33) but only for worship. It typified Christ in two ways. First, at Jesus' birth the wise men presented Him with frankincense (Mt. 2:11), emblematic of His pure life. The incense is a picture of Jesus' life, which manifested the sweet fragrance of perfection in all that He said and did. Second, the incense is a symbol of Christ through Christians. Paul said, "Now thanks be unto God, who always causeth us to triumph in Christ, and maketh manifest the savor of his knowledge by us in every place. For we are unto God a sweet savor of Christ" (2 Cor. 2:14–15).

The Offerers

Meal offerings were to be brought voluntarily to the Lord, "when any will offer" (v. 1). The offerers could bring as much meal, as often as they desired, to the Lord. The meal offering, like the burnt offering, was "a sweet savor unto the LORD"(v. 2).

The Israelites were to present their meal offerings to the priests: "And he shall bring it to Aaron's sons, the priests" (v. 2). The entire offerings were then given to the priests at the entrance to the Tabernacle. Unlike the burnt offering, no ceremony accompanied the meal offering. The Israelites did not participate in the offerings; they simply yielded their gifts to the priests in obedience to the law, picturing the Israelites presenting the fruits of their labor to the Lord. Believers today are to offer their lives and labors as living sacrifices to the Lord. Christians are to labor together in love, not for earthly rewards but for treasure that will accrue to them in heaven (Mt. 6:19–24). Realizing their labors are not in vain gives believers the incentive to be steadfast, unmovable, always abounding in good works, for they know they will someday stand before the judgment seat of Christ to have their works judged (1 Cor. 3:12–13; 2 Cor. 5:10).

The Officiating Priests

The priests took a handful of flour, cake, or grain to burn on the altar as a memorial (v. 2). The handful offered on the altar represented the whole offering presented to the Lord. The remainder of the meal offering could be eaten by the priests in the holy place or the Tabernacle court (Lev. 6:16). Only males were permitted to partake of this offering (Lev. 6:18), while the daughters of the priests were permitted to eat the other offerings, which could be taken out of the Tabernacle. For the priests to partake, they had to be ceremonially clean, for "everyone that toucheth them shall be holy" (Lev. 6:18). Likewise, Christians are expected to have a holy walk (1 Pet. 1:14–16) if they want to have communion with Christ and be used by Him. Christians are expected to feed upon Christ, who is the bread of life, receiving in return the spiritual sustenance needed for fruitful service. Jesus said, "without me ye can do nothing" (Jn. 15:5). Paul understood our great need for Christ when he wrote, "I can do all things through Christ, who strengthened me" (Phil. 4:13).

The priests were required to present a meal offering at their installation into the priesthood. They were to take a "tenth part of an ephah of fine flour," mix it with oil, and bake it in a pan. Half was offered with the burnt offering during the morning sacrifice and half during the evening sacrifice. The offerings were to be given perpetually during the time of the priests' service. They could not eat the meal offering that they presented to the Lord but were to offer it all on the brazen altar (vv. 20–23).

Although the meal offering was not a blood sacrifice, and the Israelites were permitted offer meal for a sin offering (Lev. 5:11), they still had to bring a blood sacrifice to atone for sin. Scripture definitely teaches that "it is the blood that maketh an atonement for the soul" (Lev. 17:11).

The meal offering always accompanied the burnt offering as a memorial of thanksgiving to the Lord, but there was one exception. The meal offering could be substituted for a blood sacrifice under only one condition. If an Israelite was too poor and could not afford the very inexpensive offering of two turtledoves or two young pigeons, then, and only then, could a tenth part of an ephah of fine flour be brought as a sin offering (Lev. 5:11–13). But it had to be offered without oil or frankincense, showing that it lacked the character of the usual meal offering. The reasons for this were the same as for the burnt offering.

The Israelites brought their meal offerings in thanksgiving to God for His love and mercy bestowed on them. Although Christians do not present meal offerings, they are to offer their lives and labors to the Lord. This truth is vividly expressed in Frances Havergal's hymn, "Take My Life, and Let It Be." While visiting a friend in England, she was instrumental in leading ten people in the home to salvation or recommitment to the Lord. On February 4, 1874, too happy to sleep, Frances passed the night in consecrated renewal before the Lord. As she did so, the phrase "Take my life, and let it be" came to mind, causing her to write the hymn. The last stanza goes like this,

> Take my love, my God, I pour
> At Thy feet its treasure store;
> Take myself and I will be
> Ever, only, all for Thee,
> Ever, only, all for Thee.

Is that your prayer, my friend? Why not offer your life and labor to the Lord today!

And if his oblation be a sacrifice of peace offering, if he offer it of the herd, whether it be a male or female, he shall offer it without blemish before the Lord. And he shall lay his hand upon the head of his offering, and kill it at the door of the tabernacle of the congregation: and Aaron's sons, the priests, shall sprinkle the blood upon the altar round about.

Leviticus 3:1–2

CHAPTER 13

The Peace Offering
(Leviticus 3; 7:11–21)

People have talked a lot about peace over the centuries, but they have experienced precious little of it. It has been estimated that in the last 5,600 years there have been 14,531 wars and only 292 years of world peace. The hearts of people worldwide long for peace!

Shalom is the greeting most often heard in Israel. It is translated *peace* in English, but its use is much broader in the Jewish Scriptures. *Shalom* is translated *whole* (Dt. 27:6), *finished* (Dan. 5:26), *full* (Gen. 15:16), *make good* (Ex. 21:34), *welfare* and *well* (Gen. 43:27), and *perfect heart* (1 Chr. 29:19). Solomon prayed for the people of Israel, "Let your heart, therefore, be *perfect* with the LORD our God" (1 Ki. 8:61), referring to a wholehearted commitment to the Lord. The underlying thought of *Shalom* is *health, welfare, wholesomeness,* and *harmony with God.*

The third offering in the sacrificial system was the peace offering. The Hebrew word for *peace offering (shelamin)* like *Shalom* expresses two main ideas. First, it represented sacrificial gifts brought by the Israelites in thanksgiving for the peace, friendship, and fellowship they experienced with God. Second, the peace offering, after it had been presented to the Lord, provided a fellowship meal that the Israelites and priests joyfully shared before the Lord (Dt. 12:7, 18: 14:23, 26; 15:20), God's portion having been burned on the altar.

The Offerings

The Israelites could present a bull, a cow (v. 1), a lamb (v. 7), or a goat (v. 12) as a peace offering, which differed from the burnt offering in a number of ways. First, the Israelites could choose the type of animals they presented, because God's primary intent in the sacrifice was to provide food for the sacrificial meal. Second, birds were not permitted to be sacrifices in the peace offering because no fat was to be burned on the altar, nor was there sufficient meat to feed the parties involved in the sacrificial meal. Third, there was no sex distinction in the peace offering (v. 6). The reason is not mentioned in Scripture, but possibly male animals, which were superior in worth, power, and excellence, were used for the higher and more important sacrifices. Fourth, the animals in the burnt offering were entirely consumed on the altar, but in the peace offering only the fat and kidneys were offered to the Lord (vv. 3–4, 9–10, 14–16).

The Offerers

The offerers performed the same ritual for the peace offering as for the other blood sacrifices. They led the animals to the door of the Tabernacle and laid or pressed their hands on their heads (vv. 2, 8, 13), identifying with the sacrifices as their substitute-the animals were substituting their lives for those of the Israelites. They had to bring the offerings themselves, not by proxy (7:29–30). Then they killed the animals by drawing a sharp knife across their throats. After the sacrifice was made, the Israelites took the breast and right shoulder (7:34) to be waved before the Lord (7:30). The priests placed their hands beneath those of the offerers, who held the pieces to be waved. The "wave breast" (7:34) was moved horizontally backward and forward before the

Lord, and the "heave shoulder" (7:34) was swung vertically up and down before the Lord.

Although the pieces were not burned on the altar, they were consecrated to the Lord in the method described. The priests ate the wave breast, which was symbolic of love and affection, and the heave shoulder, which symbolized strength (7:31–32, 34). The maintenance of the Levitical priesthood was carefully provided for under the law through the offerings and tithes of the people, the laborer being worthy of his hire (Lk. 10:7; 1 Cor. 9:13).

The offerers could relate to the peace of God in a number of ways. First, one of the names of God, *Jehovah-shalom* (Jud. 6:24), speaks of the perfect peace He possesses in Himself. Second, God's thoughts toward people are always of peace (Jer. 29:11), and they can experience His peace (Isa. 26:12) through faith and obedience to His commands. The key to continual blessing and peace for Israel, individually and nationally, was to walk in the statutes and commandments of the Lord (Lev. 26:3, 6). Third, the priestly benediction included a prayer to God to bestow peace on Israel (Num. 6:26). Fourth, the Israelites knew that during the kingdom age, peace would flow from Jerusalem to the whole world (Isa. 66:12).

The peace offering typified a greater fulfillment in Christ and His ministry. It was prophesied of Jesus before His birth that He would come to guide His people in the way of peace (Lk. 1:78-79). At His birth, the angelic host of heaven proclaimed peace on earth (Lk. 2:14). He bestowed peace on those He healed (Mk. 5:34) and forgave (Lk. 7:50) during His ministry. Near the end of His ministry, Christ stood looking over Jerusalem, as tears streamed down His cheeks, and said, "If thou hadst known, even thou, at least in this thy day, the things which belong unto thy peace! But now they are hidden from thine eyes" (Lk. 19:42). They had missed their day of peace through Him.

Christ made peace between God and mankind through His ministry of reconciliation: "And, having made peace through the blood of his cross, by him to reconcile all things unto himself— by him" (Col. 1:20). The word *reconciliation* means to *change,* referring to mankind's relationship with God. God is not reconciled to mankind; mankind is reconciled back to God through Christ's sacrificial death on the cross (2 Cor. 5:18-20). People will never experience peace in life until they have been reconciled to God through Jesus Christ.

The peace of believers through reconciliation is expressed in three ways. First, they have made peace *with* God (Rom. 5:1; Eph. 2:14–17); second, they have received peace *from* God (Rom. 1:7)— the true peace that can come only from God; third, the peace *of* God (Phil. 4:7; Jn. 14:27; 16:33) is the portion of every believer who walks uprightly before Him. In the future, peace on earth will be experienced by all believers when Christ, "The Prince of Peace" (Isa. 9:6), comes to establish it. Isaiah said, "Of the increase of his government and peace there shall be no end" (Isa. 9:7).

When Peter took the gospel to the Gentiles, he went "preaching peace by Jesus Christ" (Acts 10:36), telling them that God's peace was experienced only through grace by faith in Christ's finished work on the cross.

Paul often spoke of "peace from God" in the salutations and conclusions of his letters.

The Officiating Priests

As with the burnt offering, the priests caught the blood that gushed from the animals. They then sprinkled the blood on and around the altar (3:2). The priests flayed the animals, meticulously dividing them into the proper pieces, then examined the pieces for blemishes or disease.

The ritual burning of the peace offering differed from that of the burnt offering. The whole animal was consumed in the burnt offering, but only the fat and certain parts of the peace offering were burned on the altar (vv. 3–5, 9–10, 14–17; 7:3, 23). The fat from the abdominal cavity, kidneys, liver, and rump (tail) was burned on the altar.

Burning fat on the altar was of great importance in biblical times, because fat was a sign of an animal's health and vigor, being the richest part of the animal; thus, it was offered to God on the altar. The fat was placed on top of the burnt offering on the fire. The burnt offering served as the foundation of the peace offering. When placed on the altar, it was extremely flammable and quickly consumed by the fire. The tail of some sheep was very fat, weighing as much as eight to ten pounds, and was consumed the moment it was put on the altar. The fat of an animal that had died naturally or had been killed by another animal could not be burned on the altar but was used for other purposes (7:24).

Unlike the burnt offering, which was entirely consumed on the altar, three parties partook of the peace offering. First, the fat that was consumed on the altar was called "the food [bread] of the offering . . . unto the LORD" (v. 11). Naturally, the term *food for God* was not to be taken literally, because God needs no food! The fat presented to God was His share in the feast, with the priests and the people, as "a sweet savor unto the LORD" (v. 5). It was called "a sweet savor" (acceptable and well pleasing to God) because it was not offered with respect to the sin and trespass offerings. Paul spoke of Christ's sacrificial work as "a sweet smelling savor" (Eph. 5:2), referring to His voluntary obedience to the will of the Father and His death on the cross ascending as a sweet aroma before God.

The portion of the priests, consisting of the breast and right shoulder (7:34), was to be eaten for sustenance, not as a ceremonial act.

That which remained after God and the priests received their portions went to the offerers and their families. Specific restrictions regarding the sacrificial eating set the Israelites apart from other nations (Dt. 12:17–18).

The peace offering meal was a communion supper between God and the Israelites. Likewise Christians, as believer-priests, gather around the communion table in fellowship with one another, remembering Christ's sacrificial work on the cross (1 Cor. 11:23-26). It is a time of thanksgiving and joy, as believers reflect on and rejoice in the reconciling ministry of Jesus Christ, who made peace possible between God and man.

The Offerings Presented

Three types of peace offerings could be presented to the Lord (7:11–21). The first was the thanksgiving offering (7:11–15), and three kinds of bread were to be offered with it: "unleavened cakes mixed with oil, and unleavened wafers anointed with oil, and cakes mixed with oil, of fine flour, fried" (7:12). In addition to the cakes, leavened bread was to be offered. The unleavened cakes pictured the sinless Christ, who provides peace for believers, reconciling them back to God (Eph. 2:13–18), whereas the leavened bread was a thanksgiving offering for the peace God provided for them. Leavened bread typifies that believers have made peace with God through a proper sacrifice, but evil still exists in them. A part of the oblation was taken to be used as a heave offering. The word *oblation (masseath)* means *that which is carried or borne* and describes the sacrifices carried to the Tabernacle by the Israelites to be offered as a peace offering of thanksgiving. It also expressed the purpose of the sacrifice, which was to bear sin (Ex. 28:38; Lev. 10:17; 16:21). The word *heave* comes from a Hebrew word *(terumah)*, which means to be *lifted up* toward heaven by the priest. The Israelites did it in faith, showing their thanksgiving and gratitude to God as the source of all blessings. The offering was to be eaten by the priests on the same day.

The second type of peace offering was the vow offering (7:16), which was made with a vow when a person was in danger or distress to gain divine guidance and deliverance from trouble. From the moment a vow was made, Israelites were bound by obligation to perform the promised vow; thus, it was not presented voluntarily.

The third type of peace offering was the voluntary (free-will) offering (7:16). No specific time or occasion was set for this offering; Israelites could bring their offerings in appreciation to God at any time.

The vow and voluntary offerings may have been inferior to the thanksgiving offering. In the thanksgiving offering, the animals were to be eaten on the same day (7:15), but the animals of the vow and voluntary offerings could be eaten on the following day (7:16); however, none could be eaten on the third day (7:17–18). Most likely this was because by that time the meat had decayed and was impure for consumption. If any of the meat remained after the third day or touched any unclean thing, it was to be burned immediately (7:18–19).

If the Israelites or priests were ceremonially unclean (see Lev. 11—16) and ate of the sacrifice, they were "cut off from his people" (7:21). The same is true of Christians. They cannot expect to have daily communion with God if known sin remains in their lives (1 Jn. 1:6–7). Before believers partake in communion at the Lord's table, they must examine themselves and judge known sin by repenting of it, so that they can eat in fellowship with God (1 Cor. 11:27–32). Paul admonished that those who partake of the Lord's supper with sin in their lives may suffer weakness, sickness, or even death (1 Cor. 11:30).

Christians must examine their hearts daily, confessing known sin (1 Jn. 1:9), if they want to walk with God in fellowship and peace. Believers who walk with cleansed lives will experience the overwhelming "peace of God, which passeth all understanding" (Phil. 4:7).

In 1874, Frances Havergal captured the concept of God's perfect peace when she wrote:

> Like a river glorious
>   Is God's perfect peace,
> Over all victorious
>   In its bright increase;
> Perfect, yet it floweth
>   Fuller every day,
> Perfect, yet it groweth
>   Deeper all the way.
>
> Stayed upon Jehovah,
>   Hearts are fully blest;
> Finding, as He promised,
>   Perfect peace and rest.

And the Lord spoke unto Moses, saying, Speak unto the children of Israel, saying, If a soul shall sin through ignorance against any of the commandments of the Lord concerning things which ought not to be done, and shall do against any of them; If the priest that is anointed do sin according to the sin of the people, then let him bring for his sin, which he hath sinned, a young bullock without blemish unto the Lord for a sin offering.

Leviticus 4:1–3

faulty theology:
Romans 5:13 says sin is not taken into account when there is no law. i.e. there is no pinpointing details & definition. Before Newton came to understand & define gravity in mathmatical & human terms - the force of gravity existed - affected everything + its affects were real. Sin is a force, reality in mankind since Adam & Eve + it's accountability which indiudually before ToRAH was given on Sinai. many Bible proofs - beginning w/ cain
— was warned by God - Punished by God - felt guilty - held accountable (Gen 4:6-13)
— If man not accountable for sin → why did God destroy all the "sinners" - "wicked" mankind + preserve only Noah who was rignteous. (Genesis 6)

CHAPTER 14

The Sin Offering
(Leviticus 4; 6:24–30)

When Adam sinned, he brought spiritual and physical death on the human race. All die—rich or poor, strong or weak, young or old, schooled or unschooled—"it is appointed unto men once to die" (Heb. 9:27). Death reigned from Adam to Moses though individual guilt, because sin had not yet been imputed to mankind. People were not held individually accountable for their sins, because the law had not been given imputing personal guilt (Rom. 5:13). Because everyone dies, it is evident that everyone must possess a sin nature inherited through Adam. Scripture bears testimony to that fact: "every imagination of the thoughts of his heart was only evil continually" (Gen. 6:5); "there is none that doeth good, no, not one" (Ps. 14:3); "The heart is deceitful above all things, and desperately wicked" (Jer. 17:9).

Mankind became conscious of personal sin, with its accompanying guilt and consequences, when the law was given: "for by the law is the knowledge of sin" (Rom. 3:20; cp. Rom. 7:7). Although God established personal responsibility for sin through the law, He also provided an offering for that sin. Naturally, the sin offering was established to atone for a person's sin, but it taught people the seriousness of sin—the need for repentance and the consequences that unrepented sin would bring.

Although the need to expiate sin was strongly implied through the burnt and peace offerings, a special sin offering was still necessary. The sin offering was the foundation for all other offerings; without it, the Israelites could not be expiated from their sin. The sin and trespass offerings are distinguished from the other offerings, because they are non-sweet savor offerings.

The term *sin* comes from the Hebrew word *chattah* and means to *miss the mark*, or *err from God's way*. In Leviticus, *chattah* points to the act of disobedience toward God and to the sin offering by which the guilt and penalty of sin are removed.

The purpose of the sin offering was to cover sins of ignorance (v. 2) or sins committed unintentionally that come to mind (v. 28). The words *through ignorance* (Heb., *bishgagah*) [v. 2] mean to *wander, do wrong, err, sin through ignorance*. The sin offering did not cover presumptuous sins committed in rebellion against God's law and deliberately breaking His commandments (Num. 15:30–31).

The Offerings

Different animals were offered for the sin offering, depending on a person's rank in Israel. The priests (v. 3) and elders, who represented the congregation (4:13–15) were to offer a bull; a ruler, a male goat (4:22–23); and "any one of the common people" (v. 27), either a female goat (v. 28), a lamb (v. 32), two turtledoves, two young pigeons, or a tenth of an ephah of flour (Lev. 5:11).

The priests and elders were to bring a more costly offering than the rulers or common people because they were to be examples to the congregation and leaders in the nation's spiritual life. Although the rulers held a high position in Israel, they were not to be involved in representing the people before God; thus, a less expensive offering was prescribed for them. Unlike the preceding offerings, the sin offering was not voluntary but compulsory by its very nature. God's holiness demands a blood sacrifice before He can have communion with people.

The sin offering was a non-sweet savor sacrifice, because it was made with regard to sin. It typified Christ bearing the sin and shame of mankind on the cross. Both the offering and place of sacrifice were to be "most holy" (6:25) before the Lord.

The Offerers

The sin offering made clear the responsibility of the people for their sins; either a sinner bore his or her own guilt, or its penalty was paid through a blood substitute. Spiritual leaders in Israel were judged more harshly than those in lesser positions, which is shown by the prescribed ritual given to four different groups in Israel.

The Priests

The priests held the highest position in Israel, representing the people before God. The consequences of their sins were more serious and affected the entire nation (v. 3).

The priests were to bring a bull to the door of the Tabernacle and place their hands on its head (v. 4) to identify with the sacrifice as their substitute. The animals were substituting their lives for the lives of the priests. A double identification took place: The sins of the priests were committed to the animals, and the acceptability of the offerings were transmitted to the priests. The priests then killed their own offerings before the Lord (v. 4). The blood symbolically represented the offerer's own life freely surrendered. Thus, the sacrifice was accepted by God as an atonement for sin, protecting the priests from divine wrath.

The blood had to be applied in three ways for the priests and the congregation. First, the blood was sprinkled seven times in the holy place, toward the veil, in front of the holy of holies (vv.

6, 17). The sprinkled blood pictured Christ, who shed His blood and inaugurated a new and living way for believers to have access to the presence of God (Heb. 10:19–20). Second, the blood was smeared on the horns of the golden altar of incense (vv. 7, 18, 25, 30, 34), which was a place of prayer and fellowship with God. Blood from the sin offering smeared on the horns of the altar symbolized a prayer for the pardon of sin before God. Blood applied to the altar gave the incense of prayer its value. This typified Christ's blood, which gives value to the prayers of believers before God (Heb. 9:13–14; 12:24) and opens the way for them to come before the throne of grace to find mercy and grace in the time of need (Heb. 4:16). It also typified Christ as the believers' intercessor (Heb. 7:25). Third, the remaining blood was poured out at the bottom of the brazen altar (vv. 7, 18). In like manner, Christ's blood was poured out as a sin offering for mankind.

The fat and kidneys of the bull were burned on the brazen altar as a peace offering to the Lord (vv. 9–10, 19). The peace offering represented the ministry of reconciliation that Christ provided between God and mankind (Col. 1:20).

The remainder of the bull was burned outside of the camp (vv. 11–12, 21), completing the atonement for sin. The priests were permitted to partake of every offering presented on the altar except the sin offering, which was totally burned outside the camp. The bodies of the sin offerings were not burned outside the camp because they were unfit for a holy camp; in fact, just the opposite is true. An unholy camp was an unfit place for a holy sin offering.

The writer to the Hebrews showed that this was a definite type of Christ's sacrificial work on behalf of mankind. He wrote, "We have an altar, of which they have no right to eat who serve the tabernacle. For the bodies of those beasts, whose blood is brought into the sanctuary by the high priest for sin, are burned outside the camp. Wherefore Jesus also, that he might sanctify the people with his own blood, suffered outside the gate" (Heb. 13:10–12). Like the sin offering, Jesus was taken outside the gates *[handwritten annotations in top margin: "This is a big assumption." / "and erroneous he came to — Jesus said not abolish his life — paul, in the fulfill the Law — Jew all w/ messiah as bear / fulfilled as a Jew system. Jews especially persecution (camp) / lived Jewish his Lord. reproach for going mainstream messiah. / But are never accepting. commanded set aside the law"]*

of Jerusalem and suffered the fire of crucifixion, sanctifying the people with His own blood and perfectly fulfilling the picture of the sin offering in the Old Testament.

Likewise, believers must be willing to identify with Christ, "bearing his reproach" (Heb. 13:13) outside the camp. When Christ died, the Jewish system—with its laws, ceremonialism, and sacrificial system—was set aside. Today Jewish believers must go outside the camp of Judaism and identify with Christ's suffering. Many who do leave Judaism for faith in Christ suffer persecution. Paul, a classic example of a Jew suffering outside the camp, well stated, "all that will live godly in Christ Jesus shall suffer persecution" (2 Tim. 3:12).

Although the priests could not eat from their sin offerings or those of the congregation, "All the males among the priests" (6:29) could eat of the sin offering prescribed for the rulers (v. 22) and the common people (v. 27). The priests were always to be rewarded for their ministry to others. They were permitted to eat the sheep and goats, since they were not carried outside the camp to be burned, but never the bulls. The offerings could not be eaten if the blood had been sprinkled in the holy place of the Tabernacle (6:30). This applied to the offerings of the priests (v. 6) and congregation (v. 27), which were burned outside the camp (4:11–12, 21), but not those of the rulers or common people. The priests ate the sin offering in the court of the Tabernacle (6:26).

By partaking of the offering while separated from the people, the priests were reminded of their high and holy calling before the Lord (6:27). But centuries later the priests violated this commandment, polluting their holy office (Hos. 4:6–8).

The flesh and blood of the sin offering were considered holy, and those who touched them must be holy as well. If any of the blood splattered on the priests' garments, they were required to wash them in the holy place (6:27).

Special instructions were given concerning the pots in which the offerings were cooked (6:28). An earthen vessel (clay pot) had to be destroyed after one use; it could not be cleaned because the boiled flesh penetrated the pot's fiber. But the boiled flesh could be removed from a bronze pot after scouring, preserving it for future use.

The People

If the whole congregation sinned against God in ignorance, a sin offering had to be presented (v. 13). The congregation brought a bull before the Lord at the Tabernacle (v. 14). The elders, representing the people, laid their hands on the bull's head, killed it, and offered its blood as a sin offering (v. 15). The ritual for the congregation was exactly the same as for the priests (vv. 16–20), which is a type of sin in the church. The church is to judge sin immediately, or it will penetrate the whole congregation, weakening the fellowship and holding back the blessing of Gods (1 Cor. 5:1–8).

The Potentate

When a potentate, or ruler, sinned through ignorance, he was to offer a male goat (4:22–23). The offering was less than that of the priests or congregation, but greater than that of a commoner. The ritual for killing the goat was the same as for the burnt offering (v. 24). The priests sprinkled blood on the horns of the brazen altar (v. 25), but none in the holy place. Then the fat was burned as a peace offering (v. 26). The meat of the goat went to the priests only, not the people. The fact that the rulers brought a less valuable offering does not lessen their offenses compared to those of the priests or congregation. Rulers are ordained by God (Rom. 13:1–7) and will one day give an account of the way they functioned in their offices. God commands people to pray for those who rule over them (1 Tim. 2:1–2).

Individuals

When individuals sinned, they were to bring female goats or lambs without blemish (vv. 27–35) for a sin offering. The ritual of the offering was the same as those mentioned above, with one exception: the blood was not sprinkled in the holy place. If individuals were too poor, they could bring two turtledoves or two young pigeons (5:7), one for a sin offering (5:9) and the other for a burnt offering (5:10). If they were too poor for even that, they were permitted to bring "the tenth part of an ephah of fine flour for a sin offering" (5:11).

The meal offering could be substituted for a blood sacrifice, but only under one condition. If an Israelite was too poor and could not afford the very inexpensive offering of two turtledoves or two young pigeons, then, and only then, he could offer a tenth part of an ephah of fine flour as a sin offering. But it had to be offered without oil or frankincense, showing that it lacked the character of other offerings.

The oil and frankincense were removed from the meal offering for several reasons. First, this was a poor person's offering. Oil and frankincense represented costly ingredients and were not to be added. Second, this was a sin offering, and oil and frankincense, which represent fellowship with God through the Holy Spirit and prayer, were therefore to be omitted. Third, because this was a sin offering it was not to be embellished with the taste of oil or the fragrance of frankincense. The bland flour would impress upon the offerer an aversion to sin.

There were other occasions when a sin offering was to be presented, and some of the details vary, but they do not affect the underlying concept of the sin offering. The sin offering was used in the consecration of Aaron and his sons to the priesthood (Lev. 8:2, 14–15), the ceremony of purification after childbirth (Lev. 12:6–8), the cleansing of a leper (Lev. 14:12, 14, 19), the ordinance of the red heifer (Num. 19), and on the day of atonement (Lev. 16).

Since everyone in Israel sinned, the law stipulated that a sin offering had to be made. Yet animal blood, continually offered year after year, could not take away sins (Heb. 10:1–4), because the law, with all its demands, was weak through the flesh and incapable of taking away sins. For this reason, God sent Christ, in the likeness of sinful flesh, to be an offering for sin, thus condemning sin in the flesh (Rom. 8:3).

Paul succinctly showed how Christ was an antitype of the sin offering in Leviticus 4. He wrote, "For he hath made him, who knew no sin, to be sin for us, that we might be made the righteousness of God in him" (2 Cor. 5:21). Christ fulfilled the concept of a perfect sacrifice in a number of ways. First, He "knew no sin." He was the Lamb "without blemish and without spot" (1 Pet. 1:19). Jesus did not think, speak, or commit any act of sin (Jn. 8:46; 1 Pet. 2:22). Second, the sinless Christ was made sin for us. Christ did not become a sinner, but all of mankind's sins were laid on Him (Isa. 53:6), and He bore them in His own body (1 Pet. 2:24), becoming a curse when He died on the cross. It is almost beyond comprehension that God the Father would lay on the sinless Son the world's guilt and penalty of sin. Third, Christ became a sin offering so that mankind could "be made the righteousness of God in him." This is the great principle of justification. The sins of individuals are imputed to Christ, and His righteousness is imputed to believers. The sin offering cannot be expressed in a more majestic way. Believers walk away justified—declared righteous—before a holy God.

In 1865, Elvina Hall was sitting in the church choir with her head bowed as the pastor offered the morning prayer. During his prayer, four little words lingered in her mind: Jesus paid it all! Quickly she scribbled these words on the flyleaf of her hymnal, and one of the great invitational hymns of the church was born. The fourth stanza of her hymn beautifully sums up Christ's ministry on behalf of believers.

> And when, before the throne,
>   I stand in Him complete,
> "Jesus died my soul to save,"
>   My lips shall still repeat.
> Jesus paid it all,
>   All to Him I owe;
> Sin had left a crimson stain,
>   He washed it white as snow.

Yes, Jesus paid it all; all to Him we owe! But can you say, my friend, "He has washed me white as snow?"

And the Lord spoke unto Moses, saying, If a soul commit a trespass, and sin through ignorance in the holy things of the Lord, then he shall bring for his trespass unto the Lord a ram without blemish out of the flocks, with thy valuation by shekels of silver, after the shekel of the sanctuary, for a trespass offering; And he shall make amends for the harm that he hath done in the holy thing, and shall add the fifth part thereto, and give it unto the priest; and the priest shall make an atonement for him with the ram of the trespass offering, and it shall be forgiven him.

Leviticus 5:14–16

CHAPTER 15

The Trespass Offering
(Leviticus 5; 6:1–7; 7:1–7)

The trespass offering was the final Levitical sacrifice required of the Israelites. Although it was similar to the sin offering (Lev. 7:7), there were a number of differences. The sin offering dealt with sin against God; the trespass offering emphasized sin against God and mankind. The sin offering dealt with the nature of the sin; the trespass offering emphasized the acts of sin. The sin offering dealt with the guilt of the sinner; the trespass offering emphasized injury against God and mankind. The sin offering dealt with atonement (expiation of guilt); the trespass offering emphasized the satisfaction and reparation for the wrong committed.

Some commentators teach that the trespass offering began in Leviticus 5:14, because the first 13 verses in chapter 5 seem to be a continuation of chapter 4 with reference to the sin offering. This could be the case, because the sin offering is mentioned in verses 6, 7, 9, and 11. However, all of chapter 5 will be examined with reference to the trespass offering.

The word *trespass* (Heb., *asham*) means *guilt*. It denotes being guilty of infringing or violating the rights of others, whether it be God or mankind. The classic illustration of trespassing is seen during hunting season. What hunter has not seen a sign on private property reading, "No hunting: trespassers will be prosecuted?" By climbing over the fence or passing by the sign, a person is guilty of violating the property rights of another and could experience the full force of the law. So it is with the anyone who trespasses against God's law.

The Trespasser's Sins

The Israelites were to present their trespass offerings for sins committed in three areas. The first area was sins committed against *self* (5:1–13), and the first of these sins was concealing the truth (v. 1). In a Jewish court of law, a judge could adjure (summon to testify) people under oath concerning evidence they might have in a case being tried. If they refused to tell what they had seen or heard, thus withholding vital information, or lied under oath, they were guilty of concealing the truth and were therefore considered guilty of trespassing until proper atonement was made for their sins.

During Jesus' trial, Caiaphas, the high priest, adjured Him, "tell us whether thou be the Christ, the Son of God." Jesus answered Caiaphas with a prophetic statement concerning His return at the Second Coming (Mt. 26:63–64).

An application can also be made to Christians. James stated that if a believer "knoweth to do good, and doeth it not, to him it is sin" (Jas. 4:17).

The second sin was contamination by touching (vv. 2–3). The Israelites were guilty of contamination by touching dead animals, dead people, unclean lepers, or people with a discharge from their bodies. Such contamination disqualified them for worship, although they may have been unconscious of their actions. Unclean people were not able to worship before God because they were an offense to His holiness. Sin and trespass offerings were therefore required to purify the worshipers before they could come near the sanctuary in worship.

The third sin was careless talk (v. 4). If the Israelites took oaths that they later forgot or chose not to fulfill, they were guilty of sin. It made no difference whether they were good or evil oaths; the Israelites had to keep their oaths.

There are many illustrations of not keeping oaths in Scripture: Jephthah's rash vow of sacrifice to God (Jud. 11:30, 34), Saul's vow concerning eating (1 Sam. 14:24), and Peter's vow not to deny Christ (Mt. 26:33–34). Believers are to watch their words, for they will be held accountable for them before God (Mt. 12:36–37).

Before the Israelites could be restored to fellowship with God, they had to confess their sins (v. 5), admitting to the priests any of the sins mentioned with a penitential attitude and a contrite heart.

The Old Testament is filled with illustrations of true confession and contrition over sin. Two stand out very vividly: David's sin with Bathsheba (Ps. 51:4), and Achan's transgression when he took the accursed thing (Josh. 7:20–21).

Like Achan, if believers try to hide their sins, they not only bring defeat in their own lives but also affect those close to them. Christians are to confess their sins and make restitution, and God will forgive them (1 Jn. 1:9). Although confession was necessary, it did not remove the guilt of sin. A trespass offering had to be made for the guilt to be removed.

Next were sins committed against God (5:14–19). Moses revealed sins that required both a sin offering and a trespass offering, but then he focused on sins that required only a trespass offering.

Two types of transgressions could be made against holy things. First, a person could sin unintentionally (v. 15) by personally using things dedicated to God, such as tithes (Lev. 27:30; Dt. 14:22), first fruits of the harvest (Ex. 34:26), or the firstborn of cattle and sheep (Dt. 15:19). These gifts were used to maintain the priests and Tabernacle. Second, they could know the commandments but be unaware of breaking them (5:17). These sins were committed ignorantly (5:15), either by mistake or forgetfulness, and unknowingly (5:17). No trespass offering was provided to cover presumptuous sins, in which people rebelled deliberately against God's law, breaking His commandments (Num. 15:30–31; Heb. 10:26–28).

Finally, there were sins against mankind (6:1–7). The Israelites could sin against one another in five specific areas, the first being distrustfulness: if a person "lie unto his neighbor in that which was delivered him to keep" (Lev. 6:2). This could refer to something loaned by a neighbor, something left in the care of a neighbor while a person is away, or a trust made with a neighbor. People could misplace, mistreat, or misappropriate things and be guilty of trespassing against their neighbors (Ex. 22:7-11). In the New Testament, Paul taught Christians, "it is required in stewards, that a man be found faithful"(1 Cor. 4:2).

The second sin was dishonesty between partners by lying "in fellowship" (Lev. 6:2), referring to dishonesty in social and business dealings, such as unscrupulous transactions, intentionally cheating a partner out of part of the business or profit, or failure to pay an obligation, whether it be a business loan or things charged (Lev. 19:35–36). Believers today are required to "Provide things honest in the sight of all men" (Rom. 12:17) and are not to be "slothful in business" (Rom. 12:11).

The third sin was acquiring by despoiling, that is, taking from someone "by violence" (6:2). This refers to robbery, either directly, through twisting the law to one's own benefit, or by using prestige, power, or position. A classic illustration was when Ahab took Naboth's vineyard (1 Ki. 21:1–25). Believers are to have nothing to do with violence, nor are they to associate with violent people.

The fourth sin was deceiving a neighbor (6:2) or getting something by oppressing someone else. This could be done in a number of ways, such as being two-faced, through extortion, or by withholding something rightfully due another, such as wages.

The fifth sin was denial of property, whereby someone "found that which was lost, and lieth concerning it, and sweareth falsely" (6:3; cp. Ex. 22:11; Dt. 22:2–3). It is the epitome of covetousness for a person to defraud a neighbor out of something found or borrowed that belongs to that neighbor.

The phrase *sin through ignorance* is not mentioned in this section. When people sin against others, it is deliberate. Such sins can be summed up in the following proverb: "These six things doth the LORD hate; yea, seven are an abomination unto him: A proud look, a lying tongue, and hands that shed innocent blood, An heart that deviseth wicked imaginations, feet that are swift in running to mischief, A false witness that speaketh lies, and he that soweth discord among brethren" (Prov. 6:16–19).

Although the five specific sins mentioned are against other people, they are still sins against God (6:2). Two incidents in Scripture illustrate this. After David sinned against Bathsheba and Uriah, he said, "I have sinned against the LORD" (2 Sam. 12:13; cp. Ps. 51:4); when the prodigal son returned home, he confessed to his father, "I have sinned against heaven, and in thy sight" (Lk. 15:21). Thus, when sinning against a neighbor, a person also sins against God.

Christians cannot have a true walk with God and defraud their neighbors. The true character of believers is seen in their conduct toward others (Eph. 4:17–32; 5:15–16).

The Trespasser's Sacrifices

The law required that the Israelites bring their trespass (guilt) offerings to the Lord for sins against themselves (5:6–13). The type of offering varied depending upon an individual's wealth. A female lamb or goat could be brought (v. 6), but if poverty prevented such an offering, two turtledoves or two young pigeons were acceptable (v. 7). Two birds were required, one as a sin offering and the other as a burnt offering (v. 7; cp. Lev. 1:14–17).

The offering of fowl was handled differently from the animal sacrifices. The offerers were not required to lay hands on the heads of the birds or kill them; that was the priests' ministry. A bird was killed by wringing off its head (v. 8). The crop and feathers were removed and cast on the ash heap near the east side of the altar; then the bird was cut down the center and spread open, although not divided (v. 8), in order to remove the insides. Some blood was sprinkled on the altar, and the rest was wrung out at the bottom for a sin offering (v. 9).

If an Israelite was too poor and could not afford the inexpensive offering of two turtledoves or two young pigeons, then, and only then, a tenth part of an ephah of fine flour could be offered as a sin offering. But it had to be offered without oil or frankincense, showing that it lacked the character of other offerings (v. 12).

In His mercy and grace, God made exceptions even for the poor; poverty would not prevent the Israelites from receiving pardon for their sins. So it is today. Rich or poor, it makes no difference—all people can have their sins pardoned through Christ's all-sufficient sacrifice offered once (Heb. 9:28) as a sin and trespass offering. It was not by silver or gold, but through His precious blood (1 Pet. 3:18), that He provided reconciliation with God the Father.

The law required the Israelites to bring their trespass offerings to the Lord for sins committed against the holy things of the Lord (v. 15). In this instance, the trespass offering had to be "a ram without blemish out of the flock" (v. 18). The procedure for offering the ram was similar to that of the sin offering (Lev. 7:7). The law of the offering was spelled out in Leviticus 7:1–7. The Israelites brought their rams to the court of the Tabernacle, laid hands upon their heads, confessed their sins over them, presented them to the priests, and killed them. The priests caught the blood in a bowl and sprinkled it on the inner sides of the altar (7:2), as with the burnt offering and peace offering. The blood of the trespass offering was not placed on the horns of the altar, like that of the sin offering. Most likely, this was to differentiate between the expiation provided in the sin offering and the satisfaction accomplished by the trespass offering. The kidneys, fat, and rump (7:3–4) were burned on the altar by the priests for a trespass offering (7:5). The remainder of the sacrifice was for the priests and their sons as a provision in the ministry and was to be eaten in the Tabernacle.

The law required that the Israelites bring their trespass offerings to the Lord for sins against their fellowmen (6:6), but there was a change in the order of sacrifice and restitution for the trespass against mankind. In this instance, the restitution was made to the offerer first, and then the sacrifice was offered. The reason for this change was that when the sin was against God, the sacrifice came first, since blood had to be applied to atone for the sin. But when the sin was against a person, restitution had to be paid before the offering was made, because the offenders could be restored to fellowship with God only after they had been forgiven by the offended person (Mt. 5:23–24; 6:15).

Isaiah the prophet presented the Messiah as a trespass offering when he wrote, "Yet it pleased the LORD to bruise him; he hath put him to grief. When thou shalt make his soul an offering for sin" (Isa. 53:10). The word for *offering* is *asham*, the same word used in Leviticus 5—6 for *trespass* offering. In Isaiah 53:10, Christ became a trespass offering to make restitution by paying the debt of sinners to God, who had been violated; thus, He provided the required compensation necessary to satisfy God so that mankind could be reconciled back to Him.

The ram was a type of Christ's substitutionary sacrifice, dying in the sinner's place, paying the price and penalty for sin. There is a twofold description of Christ's substitutionary ministry in the New Testament. First, Christ came "to give his life a ransom *for* many" (Mt. 20:28). The word *for* indicates that Christ died *in the place of* or *instead of* the sinner. Second, "For Christ also hath once suffered for sins, the just *for* the unjust, that he might bring us to God" (1 Pet. 3:18). In this verse, the word *for* literally means *on behalf of* or *for the benefit of*, indicating that Christ suffered and died not only in the place of sinners but also in their interest.

A beautiful type of Christ's substitutionary ministry is seen in Abraham's offering of his son, Isaac, as a sacrifice (Gen. 22:1–14).

As Abraham raised the dagger to thrust it through Isaac, the angel of the Lord stopped him. Abraham lifted his eyes and saw a ram substitute caught in the thicket near the altar, which he then sacrificed as a burnt offering.

The Trespassers' Satisfaction

Unlike the other offerings, the trespass offering required that restitution be paid along with the ram sacrifice for sins against "holy things" (5:15–16) and fellowmen (6:5). The priests assessed the value of the rams that were offered, and the offenders paid the restitution in silver shekels. The Israelites were required to replace whatever they had withheld from God or mankind, and they had to add a fifth of the appraised value (5:16)—amounting to 20 cents on a dollar in our economy. The fifth part was actually a double tithe paid to the priests or the people offended. The Israelites could not be freed from their sins until they offered the proper animal sacrifices and paid the silver restitution for their transgressions. The Lord then forgave the Israelites "of all that he hath done in trespassing therein" (6:7).

Christians should make restitution whenever possible, whether it be against God or mankind. Some should make restitution for robbing God in their giving, misuse of time, or abuse of a gift. Others should make restitution for breaking a trust, destroying the good name of, or slandering the character of another.

The testimony of Zacchaeus (Lk. 19) is a splendid illustration of restitution. Before his conversion, he was the chief tax collector in Jericho and had become very rich by extorting high taxes from his countrymen for the Romans. But after his conversion, Zacchaeus made restitution to those he had cheated without Jesus urging him to do so. He vowed to give half of his possessions to the poor and promised to pay back fourfold to those he had extorted (Lk. 19:8).

Extortion was a trespass and required restitution of a fifth more (Lev. 6:5). But Zacchaeus considered it theft, which required four to fivefold restitution (Ex. 22:1). Zacchaeus proved that when people's hearts are right with God, they will make the required restitution to God and those they have wronged.

I would like to ask a very personal question. While reading this chapter, has God impressed upon you the need to make restitution with someone? Jesus gave very clear instructions on how we are to deal with trespasses against others (Mt. 18:15–35). He also warned, "if ye forgive not men their trespasses, neither will your Father forgive your trespasses" (Mt. 6:15). True blessing can come only when we are in proper fellowship with God and our fellowmen.

PART III
THE PRIESTHOOD

And take thou unto thee Aaron, thy brother, and his sons with him, from among the children of Israel, that he may minister unto me in the priest's office, even Aaron, Nadab and Abihu, Eleazar and Ithamar, Aaron's sons.

Exodus 28:1

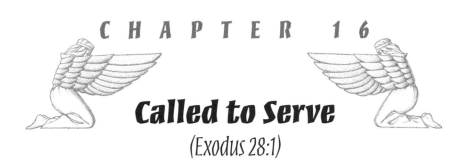

CHAPTER 16

Called to Serve

(Exodus 28:1)

Put yourself in an Israelite's position as you contemplate coming before the Lord to worship. Would you be able to enter the Tabernacle, kill the animal you brought as a sacrifice, offer its blood on the altar, and then sit down and enjoy direct communion with God? Definitely not! The Israelites never enjoyed that privilege.

The Tabernacle, with all of its beautiful furnishings, was inaccessible and of no benefit to the Israelites apart from the priesthood. Because they were unable to serve in the Tabernacle, they needed a mediating priest, someone to represent them before God. It was for this purpose that God called Aaron and his sons.

The Concept of a Priesthood

The concept of a priesthood did not originate with the nation of Israel. During the patriarchal period, the head of each household functioned as a mediating priest on behalf of his family. Job continually offered burnt offerings for each of his children, because he was afraid they may have cursed God in their hearts (Job 1:5). The first thing Noah did after leaving the ark was build an altar and offer of all the clean beasts with him a burnt offering to the Lord (Gen. 8:20). Wherever Abraham traveled through the land of Canaan, he built an altar and offered sacrifice to the Lord (Gen. 12:7–8; 13:18; 22:9). Isaac and Jacob likewise erected altars and performed the ministry of a priest before God (Gen. 26:25; 33:20).

The Choice of a Priesthood

God had delivered the Israelites from Egypt and brought them to Himself so that they would be a people for His own possession. It was God's plan that Israel be a kingdom of priests and a holy nation having direct access to Him (Ex. 19:4–6). Being priests meant that they were entitled to draw near to God in worship. Before the Aaronic priesthood was established, the head of each family, and most likely the elder son, functioned as priests, offering sacrifices on behalf of the household (Ex. 24:4–5).

Since Israel was to be "a kingdom of priests" (Ex. 19:6), God gave them the responsibility to demonstrate His standard of holiness to a world that had sunken to the depths of sin. But Israel sinned against God, breaking the covenant that He had made with them at Mount Sinai (Ex. 19:5). They forfeited the privilege of being a kingdom of priests.

It therefore became necessary for God to institute a priesthood from among the people to represent the nation of Israel before Him. While Moses was on Mount Sinai, God said to him, "And take thou unto thee Aaron, thy brother, and his sons with him, from among the children of Israel, that he may minister unto me in the priest's office, even Aaron, Nadab and Abihu, Eleazar and Ithamar, Aaron's sons" (Ex. 28:1). Thus, God chose the tribe of Levi to function as priests (Num. 3:5–13), confirming His choice by the miraculous budding of Aaron's rod (Num. 17:8).

The term *priest* (Heb., *kohen*) means *one who officiates*. Like Aaron, the priests were not chosen by the people or self-appointed; they were divinely called by God, deriving their authority directly from Him (Heb. 5:4). Christ our high priest was commissioned and sent into the world by appointment and the authority of God the Father (Lk. 4:18; Jn. 17:18; 20:21).

The priests had to be men who were able to show compassion (lit., deal gently) to the ignorant and misguided, for they themselves were beset with weaknesses of the flesh (Heb. 5:2). Priests like Caiaphas and Ananias were very cruel during their terms in office and did not exemplify the qualifications demanded for the office they held. For example, Ananias had Paul struck in the mouth, contrary to the law, for a statement he made to him (Acts 23:2–3).

God graciously provided the office of the priest so that the people, cut off from Him because of their sin, could have access to Him through a mediating priesthood. The high priest interceded for the Israelites by offering gifts (e.g., incense) and sacrifices for his own sins and those of the people (Heb. 5:1, 3).

Those chosen to serve in the priesthood could not have any physical defects. Levites were rejected for service for any of the following reasons: body blemishes, blindness, lameness, a flat nose, limbs that were deformed, a broken foot or hand, a hunchback, dwarfism, defective eyes, eczema, scabs, or being a eunuch (Lev. 21:17–21). Those rejected for service were, nevertheless, provided for because they had been born Levites (Lev. 21:22–23).

During the time of the Lord's earthly ministry, the Sanhedrin sat daily in the Hall of Polished Stones and interviewed candidates to determine if they were genealogically and physically qualified to be priests. Alfred Edersheim wrote,

> *Certain genealogies were deemed authoritative. Thus, if his father's name were inscribed in the archives of Jeshana at Zipporim, no further inquiry was made. If he failed to satisfy the court about his perfect legitimacy, the candidate was dressed and veiled in black and permanently removed. If he passed the ordeal, inquiry was next made as to any physical defects, of which Maimonides enumerates a hundred and forty that permanently and twenty-two which temporarily disqualified for the exercise of the priestly offices. Men so*

disqualified were, however, admitted to menial offices, such as in the wood chamber, and were entitled to Temple support. Those who stood the twofold test were dressed in white raiment, and their names properly inscribed. To this point allusion is made in Revelation 3:5, 'He that overcometh, the same shall be clothed in white raiment; and I will not blot his name out of the book of life . . .' (The Temple, p. 95).

A tithe system was enacted to provide for the priests and their families. The first fruit reaped by the people was given to the priests in the form of grain, fruit, wine, oil, flour, and a sheep's fleece (Dt. 18:4). A special tithe was taken every three years and given to the Levites because they had no inheritance in the land of Canaan (Dt. 14:28–29). Forty-eight cities were provided within the territories of the other tribes for the priests' habitation (Josh. 21). The firstborn from each family had to be redeemed back by paying five shekels to the priests (Num. 18:16). An unclean beast was redeemed with a set sum, which the priesthood determined, with a fifth part added to it (Lev. 27:27). The wave breast and right shoulder of a clean beast offered in sacrifice were given to the priests (Num. 18:17–18). A portion of the showbread and sacrifices was given to them for food (Num. 18:8–14). The priests received redemption money for people or things dedicated to the Lord at specific occasions (Lev. 27). A certain percentage of the spoils of war was divided among the Levites (Num. 31:25–47).

Only those who had been divinely chosen by God and were born into the tribe of Levi could serve as priests. All others who came near the Tabernacle suffered God's judgment—some were put to death (Num. 1:50–51). Korah and all those with him who had rebelled against God's choice of the Levites to be the only priests were swallowed up by the earth (Num. 16). King Saul intruded into the priest's office by offering a burnt offering and suffered the loss of his kingdom and throne (1 Sam. 13:8–14). King Uzziah was smitten with leprosy when he tried to offer incense in the Temple and remained a leper until his death (2 Chr. 26:16–21).

The Church as a Priesthood

Under the Mosaic Covenant, Israel was called to become "a kingdom of priests" (Ex. 19:6), but this priesthood was conditional. Israel had to obey the law of God to retain its position— "if ye will obey my voice," said God (Ex. 19:5). Israel failed to obey, and their standing as a kingdom of priests was dissolved. God then chose Aaron and his family to constitute the priesthood and represent the nation of Israel before Him.

When God called the church into being, He unconditionally formed it into a "kingdom of priests" (Rev. 1:6). What Israel failed to obtain as a kingdom of priests under the law, God has freely given to all believers in the church through His grace.

There are a number of parallels between the Aaronic priest and the priesthood of believers. First, Aaron was called into the priesthood; God said to Moses, "take . . . Aaron . . . that he may minister unto me in the priest's office" (Ex. 28:1). The church has been called to be a kingdom of priests (1 Pet. 2:9). Second, under the law, a man had to be born into the priesthood. Christians become priests on the basis of their birthright. By putting their trusting faith in Christ, our high priest, we are born into the family of God as adult children, assuring us of all the rights and privileges that Christ has secured for us (Jn. 1:11–13; Rom. 8:15–16; Gal. 3:26; 1 Jn. 3:1–2). Third, Aaron's sons were secure in their priesthood, not because of their own merit, but on the basis of their father's appointment as high priest. As believer-priests, we are secure in Christ, who promises that we will never be separated from our priesthood (Jn. 10:27–28; 17:2; Rom. 8:35–39).

In 1 Peter 2:9, Peter reached back into the Old Testament description of God's desire for the nation of Israel as a kingdom of priests and applied it to the church. First, the priesthood of believers is a "chosen generation" (lit., an elect race). We are a body of believers with a common descent. Our natural background of race and nationality is overshadowed by our new spiritual identity. The church is a race of people called out to show forth His praise and bring glory to His name.

Second, the priesthood of believers is a "royal priesthood" (lit., a kingly priesthood). Our position as believer-priests is far above that of the Aaronic priests, who never functioned in a kingly role, because the Aaronic priesthood was formed long before Israel had a kingly order. Believers are king-priests through Jesus Christ—not after Aaron, but after the king-priest Melchizedek. Because the whole body of believers has been formed into a kingly priesthood, there is no need for an earthly hierarchy of priests to represent believers before God. By means of His death, Jesus tore away the barrier between God and mankind, which in the past necessitated a priesthood. We now have direct access to the throne of God (Heb. 10:19–20). There is no human mediator; only the Lord Jesus Christ performs this function (1 Tim. 2:5). We are to call no one rabbi, father, or master except God the Father and Jesus Christ (Mt. 23:8–10). What an exalted position we possess. As believer-priests, we have direct access to the throne of God through Jesus Christ, His Son.

Third, the priesthood of believers is "a holy nation." As a nation of believers, we are a mixed multitude from every country of the world formed into a distinct people with the same identity. This distinct body of believers is a "holy" or *set apart* people, pilgrims and sojourners in the countries where they live (1 Pet. 1:1; 2:11). As holy, distinct people, we are called out to serve the Lord; thus, we should not desire to be like others around us in our attitudes and actions.

Fourth, the priesthood of believers is "a people of his own" (KJV, "a peculiar people"). In today's society, *peculiar* means *odd* or *strange*, but the Greek word denotes that each believer is a *unique possession of God.*" Scripture clearly states that we are not our own but have been "bought with a price" (1 Cor. 7:23), "the precious blood of Christ" (1 Pet. 1:18–19). Believer-priests today are like the nation of Israel, which was a unique possession of God.

We have not been brought into this high position as believer-priests just to enjoy the blessings of our kingship; we have a ministry to perform. Peter stated, "ye should show forth the praises of him who hath called you out of darkness into his marvelous light" (1 Pet. 2:9). The phrase "show forth the praises of him" literally means *proclaim abroad the excellencies of the Lord*, which are His glorious attributes and gracious acts toward mankind. We who are king-priests are made lights of His grace and glory and are to walk out of a dark world, dispelling the darkness by the light of our lives and testimonies.

The privilege we have as believer-priests transcends all the expectations we might envision. Ida L. Reed, who was bedridden for many years because of physical afflictions, was asked, "How do you stay so sweet amid your many trials?" She answered, "Oh, it's because I belong to the King!" The phrase stuck in her mind, and in 1896 she penned the following words:

> I belong to the King, I'm a child of His love,
> I shall dwell in His palace so fair;
> For He tells of its bliss in yon heaven above,
> And His children in splendor shall share.

We enjoy a unique privilege that the Israelites were never able to experience. As king-priests, we can come into the throne room of God through Jesus Christ and there feast in fellowship on the blessings He has for us. Child of the King, as a believer-priest, lift up your eyes to the throne of God, and let Him fill your spiritual vision. Isaiah did, and when he saw the Lord, "high and lifted up, and his train filled the temple," he heard God say, "who will go for us?" Isaiah responded, "Here am I; send me" (Isa. 6:1, 8).

Believer-priest, how are you responding to your high office?

The High Priest

THE MITRE

THE GOLDEN CROWN

ONYX SHOULDER PIECES

THE EPHOD AND ITS GIRDLE

THE BREASTPLATE

THE BLUE ROBE

BELLS AND POMEGRANATES

THE WHITE INNER ROBE

And thou shalt make holy garments for Aaron, thy brother, for glory and for beauty . . . And these are the garments which they shall make: a breastplate, and an ephod, and a robe, and an embroidered coat, a miter, and a girdle. And they shall make holy garments for Aaron, thy brother, and his sons, that he may minister unto me in the priest's office. And they shall take gold, blue, purple, and scarlet, and fine linen.

Exodus 28:2, 4–5

CHAPTER 17

Clothed for Service
(Exodus 28:2–43)

The high priest, arrayed in the stately garments of his office, methodically entered the Tabernacle to begin his day of ministry. Did it really make any difference how he dressed when representing the nation of Israel before God? Couldn't he come in garments of his own choosing, style, or design? The answers to these questions are yes and no. Yes, it did make a difference how he dressed. No, he could not come in garments of his own choosing.

God had explicitly revealed to Moses in vivid description each article of clothing to be worn by the priest. He said to Moses, "And thou shalt make holy garments for Aaron, thy brother, for glory and for beauty" (v. 2). They were to be holy because they were set apart to be worn only during the service in the Tabernacle. They were to be glorious because they exalted the priestly office in the eyes of the people. They were to be beautiful because their colors harmonized with the Tabernacle furnishings. The look of the priest was to match the function of his ministry as he worshiped God in the beauty of holiness.

The garments of the priesthood were so important that the ones chosen to make these garments were "wisehearted" (v. 3), meaning God had filled them with special knowledge and skill through the Holy Spirit so that they could make the priestly clothes. God used 43 verses to describe in minute detail how each item of clothing was to be made. Each piece of clothing is full of divine truth and spiritual teaching typical of the Lord and His ministry.

The Ephod

The term *ephod,* although a general word for *garment,* is used here in a higher sense, denoting *a special garment of religious significance.* It consisted of two pieces of material in which a thin thread of gold wire was skillfully embroidered together with blue, purple, scarlet, and fine-twined linen threads. One piece covered the chest of the high priest, and the other covered his back. The two pieces of the ephod were held together by gold-braided straps that were clasped together on the shoulders of the priest (vv. 13–14). Later in Israel's history, the ephod became the symbol of the priestly office (1 Sam. 2:28).

The gold thread running through the ephod was emblematic of the Lord's deity. The Bible explicitly states that Jesus is divine (Jn. 1:1; 20:28; Rom. 9:5), ascribing divine attributes to Him, such as His eternal existence (Rev. 1:8), omnipresence (Mt. 28:20), omniscience (Jn. 2:24–25), and omnipotence (Phil. 3:21).

The colorful materials used to make the ephod were typical of Christ's ministry. The fine-twined linen was an Egyptian white byssus yarn woven tightly together. The white speaks of purity and righteousness. Its fineness denotes the faultlessness of the material. This is a picture of Christ, who, in His flesh, was without blemish and spot (1 Pet. 1:19). The fine white linen is also a type of the saints of God who will be arrayed in fine white linen garments at the marriage of the Lamb, symbolizing their righteousness before Him (Rev. 19:7–8).

The three colors woven into the ephod were symbolic of Christ's incarnation, ministry, and second advent. The blue, probably indigo, was produced from a species of shellfish and speaks of Christ, who came down from heaven as the Son of God to do the Father's will (Jn. 3:13, 31). The scarlet was a very bright red dye produced from worms or grubs, providing a vivid picture of Christ's ministry in shedding His blood to purchase our salvation (Rom. 3:25; 5:9). The purple was produced from a secretion of the purple snail (murex). The color of royalty, purple speaks of Christ's kingship. Jesus was from the kingly line of David (Lk. 1:32), born a king (Mt. 2:2), mocked as a king (Mt. 27:29), declared to be king at His crucifixion (Mt. 27:37), and is coming back as King of kings and Lord of lords (Rev. 19:16) to rule as king forever (Lk. 1:33).

The ephod was held close to the body by a girdle (lit., belt) made of the same materials (v. 8). It was wrapped around the body of the priest and hung down to his ankles. The girdle was always used to strengthen those who wore it—a priest when he served in the Tabernacle or soldiers going off to war.

The girdle was a type of Christ, who came to minister as a servant (Mk. 10:45). At the end of His last Passover, he girded Himself with a towel and washed the disciples' feet, giving them a pointed lesson on what it meant to be a servant (Jn. 13:4–17).

Christians, as believer-priests, are to be girded with the truth of God's Word (Eph. 6:14). When the Word controls their lives, they will be able to meet the onslaughts of satanic opposition and live victorious lives in Christ. The girdle also speaks of Christians having their "loins . . . girded" and "lamps burning" (Lk. 12:35–36) in service for the Lord, while eagerly expecting His return at any moment.

The high priest wore two onyx stones, each engraved with the names of six of the 12 tribes of Israel in the order of their births. The stones were placed on the shoulders of the high priest and attached to the gold straps of the ephod (vv. 9–12). It is not known what the onyx stones were made of; they may have been one of two types. The Septuagint translation of the Bible states that the stones were emeralds. Josephus, the Jewish historian, believed that the onyx stones were sardonyx, which is a three-layered stone black, white, and red in color. The onyx stones were placed on the shoulders of the high priest to remind him that he was representing the 12 tribes of Israel before God during his ministry (v. 12). This is a beautiful type of Christ, who bears the needs of believers before the throne of God, where He intercedes for them (Heb. 7:25; 9:24; 1 Jn. 2:1).

The Breastplate

Made of the same materials as the ephod, the breastplate was square in shape and doubled over to form a pouch in the center (v. 16). Twelve precious stones were set in gold and placed in rows on the breastplate, representing the 12 tribes of Israel (vv. 17–21):

Reuben:	Sardius	**Dan:**	Sapphire	**Issachar:**	Amethyst
Simeon:	Topaz	**Naphtali:**	Diamond	**Zebulun:**	Beryl
Levi:	Carbuncle	**Gad:**	Jacinth	**Joseph:**	Onyx
Judah:	Emerald	**Asher:**	Agate	**Benjamin:**	Jasper

The breastplate was held in place by four rings, two on the corners of the plate and two on the ephod (vv. 23, 26). A braided gold cord passed through the upper rings and was attached to the settings on the shoulder stones (v. 25). A ribbon of blue lace was passed through the lower rings and sewn onto the front of the ephod a little above the girdle (vv. 26–28).

This breastplate was called "the breastplate of judgment" (lit., decision) [vv. 15, 29–30], because it contained the Urim and Thummim (v. 30) by which God was consulted to discern His will for the people. Today we must go through Jesus our high priest to discern God's will in areas of uncertainty (1 Tim. 2:5; 1 Jn. 2:1); all final judgment has been left to Him (Jn. 5:22, 27).

The high priest bore the children of Israel upon his heart, each tribe represented by a precious stone, as he ministered before the Lord (v. 29). The Lord bears us close to His heart as He represents us before God (Rom. 8:33–34). Each Christian is a precious stone to the Lord, forming His church (Eph. 2:21–22; 1 Pet. 2:5). As each stone in the breastplate had its individual character, color, beauty, and glory, so it is with Christians. Although fitly framed together in one body, we each reflect Christ's glory in our own unique way.

As priests of God, we are to put on "the breastplate of righteousness" (Eph. 6:14). A breastplate covered the vital organs of a soldier, especially the heart. We have the imputed righteousness of Christ, which guards us against the fiery darts of Satan, who tries to strike us at the heart of our faith.

The Urim and Thummim

The Urim and Thummim were in the pocket of the breastplate, resting over the heart of the high priest when he went before the Lord. The term *Urim* is mentioned seven times in the Old Testament, and *Thummim* is mentioned five times (Ex. 28:30; Lev. 8:8; Num. 27:21; Dt. 33:8; 1 Sam. 28:6; Ezra 2:63; Neh. 7:65). *Urim* means *lights,* and *Thummim* means *perfection;* both were used in seeking divine counsel and guidance from the Lord (Num. 27:21).

Many scholars have been puzzled about how the Urim and Thummim actually functioned in decision making, and their interpretations vary greatly. Although we do not know exactly how the Urim and Thummim functioned, we do know that they were used in determining the will of God for the Israelites, which is the important thing.

The Urim was a beautiful picture of Christ, who is the believers' light. He said, "I am the light of the world; he that followeth me shall not walk in darkness, but shall have the light of life" (Jn. 8:12). This "light of life" can be obtained only by putting faith in His atoning work on the cross. Jesus made it very clear that the world in general will not come to Him as the light of life: "And this is the condemnation, that light is come into the world, and men loved darkness rather than light, because their deeds were evil" (Jn. 3:19). True believers can have the perfect light of God's will through Jesus Christ (Jn. 14—16). The Thummim speaks of the perfection found in Christ (1 Pet. 2:22). He is our perfect counselor (Col. 2:3) and lights the path we are to tread as He guides us along the way.

The Robe of the Ephod

The robe was a blue, seamless garment with slits in the sides for the arms and a hole in the top for the head. It was reinforced so that it would not fray or tear. The robe reached to just below the knees of the high priest and was trimmed with pomegranates of blue, purple, and scarlet to harmonize with the other pieces of the priestly garments. The pomegranates were alternated with pure gold bells.

The colors in the pomegranates were symbolic of Christ's heavenly origin, incarnation, ministry, and second advent. They speak of the fruitfulness produced by Christ's sacrificial work on the cross (1 Cor. 15:23). The bells speak of testimony. The sounding of the bells united the people and the high priest as he ministered. Through the sounding of the bells, the people were able to follow the priest's movements and be in prayer with him.

The Miter

The headdress worn by the high priest was the miter (v. 37). *Miter* means to *wrap* or *roll around.* Josephus said that the headdress was like a crown made of thick linen swathes wrapped around the head of the high priest, similar to a turban (Ant. Jud. 111:7:3). A plate of pure gold engraved with the words "HOLINESS TO THE LORD" (v. 36) was placed on blue lace and tied to the front of the miter (v. 37). It served a twofold purpose. It indicated, first, that the high priest was to "bear the iniquity of the holy things, which the children of Israel shall hallow in all their holy gifts" (v. 38). The word *bear* means to *carry away.* The high priest was to carry away the iniquities of the people by the atonement made through the blood of the sacrifice (Lev. 10:17). Second, the gold plate was to "be always upon his forehead" (v. 38) so that the Israelites would be accepted before the Lord. This is a beautiful picture of the Lord's ministry. He did not wear the words "HOLINESS TO THE LORD," but He is the holy Lord. As our high priest, Jesus, who is holy, offered Himself as a sacrifice, not just to bear our iniquities but to once and for all take them away "by the sacrifice of himself" (Heb. 9:26). In Christ we are made righteous and holy (2 Cor. 5:21).

As believer-priests, we offer "spiritual sacrifices" to God through Jesus Christ (1 Pet. 2:5). The gold plate on the miter reminds us that, as believer-priests, our lives and service are to be holy. Peter wrote, "But, as he who hath called you is holy, so be ye holy in all manner of life, Because it is written, Be ye holy; for I am holy" (1 Pet. 1:15–16).

The Breeches and Undergarments

The breeches (drawers) made from linen were to cover the nakedness of the priest from the loins to the thighs (v. 42). Many of the nations surrounding Israel did not cover their priests as the Israelites did. In fact, much of the heathen worship of the ancient world was sensual and obscene, with services performed naked by the people. But God demanded that worship to Him be carried out in modesty and decency. The priests were to "worship the LORD in the beauty of holiness" (Ps. 29:2; 96:9).

This should convict us, as believer-priests, to be sure that our manner of dress is glorifying to God when we come before Him in worship. The Scriptures give explicit instructions to women concerning how they should dress (1 Tim. 2:9–10; 1 Pet. 3:3), and the same applies to men.

A coat (lit., tunic) was worn under the outer clothing of the high priest. Josephus stated that it had tight-fitting sleeves and reached down to the feet (Ant. Jud. 3:7:2). The tunic was held in place by a girdle of needlework (Lev. 8:7).

The Garments of the Priests

The garments described thus far were those of the high priest. A description is also given of the ministerial garments worn by other priests who served in the Tabernacle. They wore a coat, miter, girdle, and breeches made of fine linen "for glory and for beauty" (vv. 40–42), but the style and pattern differed from that of the high priest, being much simpler.

In the Scriptures, garments have always been a symbol of righteousness. As believer-priests, we have been clothed with the white garment of salvation and robed in righteousness, as a bride adorns herself for her marriage (Isa. 61:10). Because we are clothed with Christ's righteousness, Paul instructed us to put off the old life of sin, as one strips away an old, worn-out suit of clothes (Col. 3:8–9).

Believer-priests are not to allow their garments (under tunic) to be spotted by the flesh (Jude 23). As a garment can be spotted by the flesh it touches, so Christians can be defiled by the things in the world that touch them; thus, we are to keep ourselves from the corruption of the world by setting our affections on things above (Col. 3:1–2). By being clothed in the righteous knowledge of Christ, we are empowered through the Holy Spirit to live victorious, fruitful lives in the Lord (Col. 3:10). We await that great day when the old sin nature will be stripped away, and we will stand before the Lord clothed in white raiment. John said that at the marriage supper of the Lamb we will "be arrayed in fine linen, clean and white" (Rev. 19:8). The white linen represents the righteous deeds that were manifested by believers during their earthly ministries.

We who have been clothed in His righteousness are fit for worship and service. We are to go forth from worship to serve in this dark world, manifesting the glory and beauty of Christ through our lives.

Do others see the glory and beauty of Christ shining through your life?

And Moses took of the anointing oil, and of the blood which was upon the altar, and sprinkled it upon Aaron, and upon his garments, and upon his sons, and upon his sons' garments with him; and sanctified Aaron, and his garments, and his sons, and his sons' garments with him.

Leviticus 8:30

CHAPTER 18

Consecrated for Service

(Exodus 29; Leviticus 8)

A hush fell over the congregation of Israel as they gathered before the Tabernacle. Excitement pounded in the hearts of the Israelites as they anticipated the events that were about to unfold. Patiently they waited for the emergence of the man whom God had called to represent them as high priest. Muffled sounds of excitement were heard as Aaron appeared for the first time clothed in the beautiful garments of the high priest. Unlike the hidden rites of the pagan religions surrounding Israel, Moses consecrated Aaron and his sons to the priesthood in full view of the people (Lev. 8:3–5).

Cleansed for Service

The consecration began with Moses thoroughly washing Aaron and his sons at the door of the Tabernacle (Ex. 29:4; Lev. 8:6). This was the only time that a priest was washed by another; henceforth, he washed himself in preparation for daily service (Ex. 30:19–20).

Washing had a twofold meaning. First, it typified the priests' regeneration. As believer-priests, Christians have been "saved . . . by the washing of regeneration, and renewing of the Holy Spirit" (Ti. 3:5).

Second, like the high priest, Christians must be cleansed from daily sins (1 Jn. 1:9). The need for daily cleansing was clearly illustrated in the final hours of the Lord's earthly ministry when He washed His disciples' feet (Jn. 13:1–10). Jesus said to Peter, "He that is washed needeth not except to wash his feet" (v. 10). The two words for *wash* in this verse have different meanings. The word *washed (Gr., louo)* means to *bathe the body completely.* It speaks of our complete ablution, which took place at the moment of regeneration. The word *wash (Gr., nipto) is* used for those who *wash their hands and feet symbolizing daily cleansing.* Believers, having been thoroughly cleansed through the blood of Jesus Christ, must still be cleansed in their daily walk with the Lord.

Clothed for Service

Aaron and his sons were stripped of their old clothing and separately dressed by Moses after being bathed. Aaron's clothing consisted of a linen tunic, under girdle, robe of the ephod, ephod, outer girdle, breastplate, Urim and Thummim, and the miter with its gold plate inscribed "HOLINESS TO THE LORD" (Ex. 29:5–9; 40:13–14; Lev. 8:7–9). Aaron's sons were clothed in a separate service, and their garments consisted of a linen coat, miter, girdle, and breeches (Ex. 28:39–42). It is important to remember that Aaron and his sons were initially clothed by one another, rather than by themselves.

Christians do not outfit themselves for service. God calls, directs, and enables believers to serve Him (Jn. 15:16). They have been equipped by God for the tasks they are called to perform by the indwelling power of the Holy Spirit. God has clothed believers with armor to stand against the onslaughts of Satan (Eph. 6:13–17).

Consecrated for Service

The service of consecration was initiated by Moses, who poured the anointing oil over Aaron's head and sprinkled his sons. The oil was a crown (Lev. 21:12) on the head of the high priest, running down his beard to the hem of his garment (Ps. 133:2).

The anointing oil was made from a specific formula consisting of 500 shekels of pure myrrh (a gum resin extracted from the Arabian Balsamodendron Myrrha plant used in embalming), 250 shekels of sweet cinnamon, 250 shekels of sweet calamus (the aromatic bark of a shrub growing in Arabia), 500 shekels of cassia (a plant having the flavor and aroma of cinnamon), and a hin (one gallon) of olive oil (Ex. 30:22–25).

Rabbinical sources state that Moses, having reduced the solid ingredients to powder, steeped them in water until all the aromatic qualities were drawn out. The olive oil was then poured into the ingredients and the water boiled out. The residue thus obtained was preserved in a vessel for use *(Unger's Bible Dictionary, p.* 806).

In quoting Isaiah 61:1 and 2, Christ acknowledged that He had received the anointing power of the Holy Spirit in order to perform His ministry. He said, "The Spirit of the Lord is upon me, because he hath anointed me to preach the gospel to the poor; he hath sent me to heal the brokenhearted, to preach deliverance to the captives, and recovering of sight to the blind, to set at liberty them that are bruised" (Lk. 4:18). The Scriptures clearly show that Christ's total ministry was performed through the Holy Spirit (Acts 10:38).

Oil is a fitting symbol of the Holy Spirit in the lives of Christians. They have been regenerated (Ti. 3:5), baptized into the church (1 Cor. 12:13), indwelt (1 Cor. 6:19), and sealed unto the day of redemption (Eph. 1:13–14) through the Spirit's ministry. But it is the filling by the Holy Spirit that empowers Christians for service (Eph. 5:18). If believer-priests are not controlled by the Holy Spirit, their ministry will be insipid and of no effect.

The anointing oil had a sweet fragrance that permeated the one over whom it was poured, presenting a beautiful picture of Christ in His perfection and grace before God and mankind. His life emitted a fragrant perfection of purity and holiness and was unmarred by sin or fleshly motives. Christians who are anointed with the Holy Spirit emit a sweet fragrance to both God and the world. As they move through society, they emit the fragrant knowledge of Christ to the glory of God. The world responds in various ways to the fragrance of Christ. To those who are lost and indifferent to the gospel, the fragrance of Christ is "the savor of death unto death"; but to those who respond to our witness, Christ is "the savor of life unto life" (2 Cor. 2:14–17).

There were three prohibitions concerning the use of the anointing oil. First, it was to be poured only on the head and not "Upon man's flesh" (Ex. 30:32). Christians can never hope to produce the results of the Holy Spirit's anointing. Works done in the flesh are a stench in the nostrils of God. This was clearly seen when Simon the sorcerer tried to purchase the anointing power of the Holy Spirit. He was severely condemned by Peter (Acts 8:9–21).

Second, the anointing oil was not to be produced for the priests' own use or for secular purposes. Moses said, "neither shall ye make any other like it, after the composition of it: it is holy, and it shall be holy unto you" (Ex. 30:32). Neither are Christians to use the gifts of the Spirit for their own use or secular advantage. They should not try to imitate the ministry of the Holy Spirit with secular means.

Third, the anointing oil was not to be put "upon a stranger" (i.e., one not of the priesthood, Ex. 30:33). Paul stated, "Now if any man have not the Spirit of Christ, he is none of his" (Rom. 8:9). The anointing of the Spirit cannot work through unbelievers, who are strangers to the things of God.

Consecrated by Sacrifice

The sacrifice of consecration followed the anointing service, with Moses officiating as the priest (Ex. 29:10–34). Three animals were sacrificed: a young bullock for the sin offering, a ram for the burnt offering, and a ram of consecration.

The Sin Offering of Consecration (Ex. 29:10–14)

The bullock was to be readied for sacrifice before the consecration ceremony began (v. 10). This is the first scriptural mention of the sin offering; all of the preceding offerings were either burnt offerings or peace offerings. Aaron and his sons identified with the bull as their substitute by placing their hands on its head, thus transferring their personal sins to it (v. 10). Moses killed the bull, smeared its blood on the horns of the brazen altar, and poured the remaining blood at the base of the altar (vv. 11–12). The fat of the viscera and the liver along with the two kidneys with their fat were burned on the altar, but the flesh, skin, and dung were burned outside the camp of Israel as a sin offering (vv. 13–14).

The pieces of the bullock burned on the altar spoke of Christ's sacrifice on the cross being acceptable in God's sight (Isa. 53:10). The pieces burned outside the camp typified the fact that Christ took our judgment on Himself, being crucified outside the camp (Heb. 13:11–12).

The priests clearly understood that the animal died vicariously, its blood atoning for their sin, to bear the penalty and judgment that they deserved. The priests, covered by the sin offering, were then free to enter the presence of God to minister on behalf of the people.

The offering emphasized that apart from the shedding of blood there is no remission of sin (Heb. 9:22). Christ vicariously shed His blood, becoming the believer-priests' sin-bearer (2 Cor. 5:21; 1 Pet. 2:24) and opening the way for them to be prepared for service.

The Burnt Offering of Consecration (Ex. 29:15–18)

The ram for the burnt offering was brought before Aaron and his sons. Again they placed their hands upon the ram to identify with the animal as their representative (v. 15). The ram was slain and its blood sprinkled on and around the altar (v. 16). The word *sprinkle* literally means to *cast*. Rabbinical tradition holds that the blood was thrown from the basin, sprinkling the four corners, rather than being sprinkled by hand or with hyssop. The ram was cut into pieces, washed, and the whole animal burned on the altar as a burnt offering for a sweet savor to God (vv. 17–18).

The burnt offering symbolized complete, voluntary surrender to God. It is a fitting picture of Christ, who, without spot or blemish, freely offered Himself as a sacrifice unto death, fulfilling the will of God. His sacrifice was a sweet savor to God in two ways. First, He was completely devoted to doing the Father's will (Mt. 26:39). Second, His sacrifice was completely accepted by God the Father as an atonement for sin.

The sacrifice was to be offered by the voluntary will of the individual (Lev. 1:3). Believer-priests are to voluntarily offer themselves as living sacrifices to God. When they do this, it is "unto God a sweet savor of Christ" (2 Cor. 2:15).

The Ram of Consecration (Ex. 29:19-21)

The final sacrifice offered by Moses was the ram of consecration. Again, Aaron and his sons identified with the ram substitute by placing their hands on its head (v. 19). The ram was then killed, and its blood was applied to the right ears, thumbs, and large toes of Aaron and his sons (v. 20).

The blood applied to the right ears symbolized that the priests' ears were consecrated to God's service. They were to be attentive to the voice of God, which instructed them concerning the way in which they were to function and speak to the people.

The same is true of believer-priests, whose ears are to be yielded to the Lord. They are to turn a deaf ear to the alluring voice of Satan and the world, who try to persuade them to compromise their faith. The Lord closed His messages to each of the seven churches He addressed in the Book of the Revelation with the admonition, "He that hath an ear, let him hear what the Spirit saith unto the churches" (Rev. 2:7, 11, 17, 29; 3:6, 13, 22). In preparing for service, only anointed ears will be quick to respond to God's voice as He gives direction through His Word.

Anointing the right thumb with blood signified the power and skill of each individual (Ex. 15:6, 12). The priests' hands were to be sanctified to the work of the Lord. Likewise, believer-priests are to enter the ministry with clean hands (Jas. 4:8).

Anointing the large toes of the priests' right feet with blood symbolized that they were to have a sanctified walk before the Lord. The Word of God speaks often about the sanctified walk of believers. They are to sidestep the broad way of life that leads to destruction and walk down the narrow way that leads to life (Mt. 7:13–14).

In Ephesians, Paul gave believer-priests a number of guidelines to direct them in their holy walk. First, they are not to walk as the world walks—in the vanity (futility) of their minds—but as children of light, having put on the new man (regenerated man) who is patterned after God in righteousness and holiness (Eph. 4:17–32).

Second, believer-priests are to walk worthy in all humility, gentleness, patience, and forbearance to others, which can be manifested only in love. They are to eagerly guard the unity of the Spirit in their walk (Eph. 4:1–3, 30).

Third, believer-priests are to walk as witnesses, imitating God in two ways, the first of which is to "walk in love" (Eph. 5:2). The love of Christ, manifested through believers' lives, will draw men to Him. Jesus said, "By this shall all men know that ye are my disciples, if ye have love one to another" (Jn. 13:35). Another way to imitate God is to walk as "children of light" (Eph. 5:8). The fruit of this light will be manifested in goodness, righteousness, and truth through believers' lives as a witness to a lost world.

Fourth, believer-priests are to walk in wisdom, "circumspectly" (i.e., carefully) and not carelessly (Eph. 5:15). The key to doing this is knowing the "will of the Lord" (Eph. 5:17) through proper appropriation and application of God's Word. Only then will they wisely redeem the time in their walk before God, buying up the precious opportunities opened to them (Eph. 5:16). To maintain a holy walk with God, believers must be "filled [controlled] with the Spirit" (Eph. 5:18).

The blood that remained was mixed with the anointing oil and sprinkled on Aaron and his sons and on their garments (v. 21). The mixture symbolized the combined work of the blood, which justifies, and the oil of the Holy Spirit, which sanctifies.

The Wave Offering of Consecration (Ex. 29:22–46)

Moses took the rump, the fat of the viscera and liver, the two kidneys with their fat, and the right shoulder of the ram of consecration (v. 22), along with an unleavened cake, a cake of oiled bread, and a thin cake sprinkled with oil (v. 23) to be offered as a wave offering by Aaron and his sons (v. 24). Afterward, Moses received the offering from Aaron and his sons to be burned on the brazen altar as a sweet savor to the Lord (v. 25). He then took the breast of the ram, which was Aaron's consecration, and waved it before the Lord as a wave offering, and the breast became Moses' (v. 26). Aaron and his sons took the remaining flesh of the ram, boiled it at the Tabernacle door, and ate it, along with the unleavened bread that remained (vv. 31–32; Lev. 8:31–32).

Completion of the Service

Aaron and his sons repeated the ceremony of consecration for seven days (Ex. 29:35). Since seven is the number of completion, the keeping of the ceremony for seven days spoke of a complete consecration of the priests who were to represent their fellow Israelites before God.

God wants believer-priests to give themselves in complete consecration to His service. Paul wrote, "present your bodies a living sacrifice, holy, acceptable unto God, which is your reasonable service" (Rom. 12:1).

We are to present our bodies once and for all, as the Levitical sacrifice was offered to God. The sacrifice of Christians differs from the Levitical sacrifice in that it is "living" (ready to be used in God's will and for His glory). Christians' bodies become "the temple of the Holy Spirit" (1 Cor. 6:19–20), indwelt by the Holy Spirit (Rom. 8:9), to be used for God's glory (Phil. 1:20–21). This sacrifice is "holy" because it is set apart for God's service to be used in a righteous manner. It is "acceptable" because, when Christians present their bodies, God is well pleased. It is also their "reasonable service" or spiritual worship. Paul had in mind the service of believer-priests rather than the Levitical priests, who offered sacrifice only apart from themselves. Believer-priests put their bodies on the altar in worship and service to God.

You might wonder how you can offer your body to God. Each morning when you rise, before you put your feet on the floor, commit your mind, eyes, ears, hands, and feet to the Lord, asking that the members of your body be guarded from sin and used for God's glory (Rom. 6:19).

Avis B. Christiansen summed up what our commitment should be in the third stanza of her hymn, "Only One Life":

> Only one life to offer, Take it, dear Lord, I pray;
>   Nothing from Thee withholding, Thy will I now obey;
> Thou who hast freely given Thine all in all for me,
>   Claim this life for Thine own, to be used my Savior,
> Every moment for Thee.

And the Lord spoke unto Moses, saying, Speak unto Aaron and to his sons, that they separate themselves from the holy things of the children of Israel, and that they profane not my holy name in those things which they hallow unto me: I am the Lord.

Leviticus 22:1–2

CHAPTER 19

Conduct in Service
(Leviticus 21—22)

Priests did not enter their position by choice, spiritual astuteness, or the personal qualities they possessed, but by birth into the Aaronic family. However, to be accepted for service in the Tabernacle, they had to meet the stringent regulations set forth by God.

Since a priest was "a chief man among his people" (21:4), great responsibility was given to him to exemplify personal purity in his character and conduct before Israel. If he disobeyed the divine regulations of his office, he was immediately dismissed from service in the Tabernacle.

Disqualification for Service

In order for priests to be examples before their fellow Israelites, certain domestic restrictions were placed on them that were not required of the nation of Israel. Similarly, because of their priestly position, a number of privileges were denied them in their family relationships.

Funeral Rites

The priests were not permitted to defile themselves by taking part in any funeral rites (v. 1) except those legally permitted because of family ties. They were permitted legal defilement to attend the funerals of their mothers, fathers, sons, unmarried daughters, and wives (although the wife is not mentioned) [vv. 2–3]. The high priest was not permitted to interrupt his ministry even to attend the funeral of his father or mother (v. 11). This may seem rather harsh and heartless, but it must be remembered that the high priest was totally separated to the things of God by the anointing oil poured on him (v. 10).

A great deal of time would have been spent away from ministry if the priests had to officiate at the funerals of those who died in the wilderness. If a priest came in contact with a dead body, he was unclean for seven days (Num. 19:11–14).

The Lord demanded such commitment from those who would be His followers. A would-be disciple said to Him, "Lord, permit me first to go and bury my father." Jesus replied simply, "Follow me, and let the dead bury their dead" (Mt. 8:21–22). There are times when commitment to the Lord transcends even our family responsibilities and relationships (Mt. 10:37). Many have experienced this by leaving relatives and friends to serve the Lord in another city, state, or country.

Naturally, it is not wrong to mourn the death of a loved one; even the Lord did so (Jn. 11:33–36). But mourning must be done in a manner that glorifies God. Priests were prohibited from mourning, in the customs of the heathen nations surrounding Israel, by mimicking their superstitious practices or ceremonies. They were prohibited from shaving their heads, beards, or eyebrows (Lev. 19:27; Dt. 14:1) or making any cuts in their flesh (v. 5). Because the priests served the altar of the Lord, mourning in a manner that dishonored God would profane His name and the priesthood (v. 6).

It is important that believer-priests bring dignity and honor to God in the mourning of loved ones. Mourning can be a time

of witness to unbelievers of our faith in the Lord and His sufficiency to sustain us in the most difficult times of life.

Family Relationships

It was mandatory for priests to make wise choices of marriage
partners. They were prohibited from marrying "an harlot, or profane
[secular and not spiritual in her interest], neither shall they take a
woman put away from her husband [a divorcee]" (v. 7). Their wives
had to have a good testimony among the people, so that they would
not bring reproach on their husbands' ministry (v. 8).

The high priest had even greater restrictions on his choice of a
wife. She could not be a prostitute, a profane woman, a divorcee,
or a widow; she had to be a virgin (v. 14).

The bride of the high priest typified the bride of Christ,
which is the church. The church is in union with Christ as "a
chaste virgin" (2 Cor. 11:2). Although the church is not without
blemish today, it will be presented as such (Eph. 5:27) during
the marriage supper of the Lamb (Rev. 19:7–8).

Believer-priests are to be holy in their marital relationships, being
the husband of one wife (Mt. 19:4–6), who is to be an example of
holiness in marriage and the home (Ti. 2:3, 5). Marriage is to be lived
out in a way that will bring glory to the Lord. This can be accomplished only if husbands and wives fulfill their rightful roles in the
marriage relationship (Eph. 5:22–23, 25).

The conduct of the priests' children was of great importance.
Their daughters could disgrace and discredit their fathers' ministry
by immorality (v. 9). If they became prostitutes, the law required
their immediate death by burning (v. 9). Punishment was carried
out swiftly as an example to others.

The priests had a responsibility to see that their sons married
according to the law (v. 15). Failure of a priest's son to marry properly brought disgrace to the family and disqualified him from the
priesthood. This was a terrible indictment on the high priest Eli, who
allowed his two sons Hophni and Phinehas to commit adultery at
the Tabernacle (1 Sam. 2:22), causing the people to lose respect for the
priest and the Tabernacle (1 Sam. 2:17). Eli was severely judged for
neglecting to discipline his sons (1 Sam. 2:27–36).

In the same spirit, Paul instructed Christian leaders to oversee the behavior of their families (1 Tim. 3:4–5). Children in Christian homes are expected to live in obedience to their parents, not disgracing them by rebelling against their leadership (Eph. 6:1–3). Likewise, fathers are to nurture (discipline) and admonish their children in a way that will not provoke (arouse to wrath) them from following their leadership (Eph. 6:4).

Deficient for Service

Priests had to be physically fit, manifesting no deformities or blemishes, to qualify for service in the Tabernacle. They were rejected for service for blemished bodies, blindness, a flat nose, deformed limbs, a broken foot or hand, a hunchback, dwarfism, defective eyes, eczema, scabs, or being a eunuch (vv. 17–20). Although these conditions disqualified men from serving in an official capacity, they were permitted to do tasks that would not bring them near the altar (v. 23) and were allowed to eat the showbread and offerings of the Tabernacle (v. 22). Moses instructed Aaron, his sons, and the people concerning the priestly qualifications.

The perfection of the priests was a type of the Lord Jesus Christ, who had no sin, blemish, or spot (1 Pet. 1:19). If the Lord had possessed any defect, it would have been impossible for Him to provide our redemption through His shed blood (Heb. 7:26–28).

A lesson can be drawn for believer-priests from the priestly qualifications. Those serving in leadership positions in the local church must be blameless in their domestic and social relationships (1 Tim. 3). Some Christians have moral and ethical blemishes from their pasts that disqualify them from official service but not from fellowship within the body of Christ.

Defilement in Service

Priests were not to mix material objects dedicated for worship in the sanctuary (holy things of the children of Israel) with objects used in their secular lives (v. 2). Also, they had to be ceremonially clean before they could enter the sanctuary to minister. Failure to cleanse themselves meant that they forfeited the right to minister and had to be removed from the priestly office (v. 3).

Moses enumerated the various forms in which priests could be ceremonially defiled: leprosy, a running issue (gonorrhea), touching the dead, an emission of seed, touching an unclean animal or person (vv. 4–5, 8). If a priest defiled himself, he was required to wash completely, be pronounced cleansed, then wait until after sunset before being permitted to eat the Tabernacle offering (vv. 6–7). Failure to take the proper steps in removing his uncleanness might result in his death (v. 9).

Through daily communication with the world, believer-priests can become contaminated; therefore, it is necessary that they continually examine their walk (1 Cor. 11:31–32) and confess and forsake the sins that grieve the Holy Spirit, so that they can be cleansed for service. If they fail to judge their walk before the Lord, sin will destroy their spiritual lives, disqualifying them for ministry (Jas. 1:15). Their private walk is to match their public work for the Lord.

Priests were not free to share the Tabernacle food with just anyone. No stranger (layman not of the priesthood), sojourner (traveler lodging with a priest), or hired servant was permitted to eat their food (v. 10). Only those in their immediate families still residing at home, purchased slaves, or childless daughters (widowed or divorced, having returned home) were permitted to eat of the Tabernacle offerings (vv. 11–13).

An outsider's ignorance of the law did not excuse him from penalty, even if he ate the Tabernacle offering unwittingly. The law stipulated that he must restore the portion eaten plus 20 percent of its value (v. 14). These stringent regulations were established for the priests and people to make them conscious of the importance God placed on His sanctuary and its holy function. The law put the priests on constant guard concerning their approach and ministry in the Tabernacle. They could not come improperly prepared; one slip could defile and disqualify them from service.

The death of Nadab and Abihu, who offered strange fire on the altar, is a clear example of God's swift judgment on those who do not approach holy things of the sanctuary with reverence and respect (Lev. 10:1–2).

The Lord instructed believers, "Give not that which is holy unto the dogs, neither cast your pearls before swine" (Mt. 7:6). The metaphor is taken from Leviticus 22:1–16 and instructs Christians, who are stewards of the gospel, not to handle it carelessly or irreverently. They are to use discernment and not allow vile people who reject God's grace to trample on the spiritual treasure of the gospel, cheapening it. But many believers are cheapening the gospel through their attitudes and actions, thus discrediting Christ and His church. It behooves believers to be vigilant in their walk so that they will not dishonor or disgrace the Lord.

Discretion in Sacrificing

God impressed upon the people and priests the importance of the sacrifices they were to bring. The animals were to be without blemish (vv. 17–25). For humane and health reasons, they could not be offered before they were eight days old (vv. 26–27). This restriction was humane because it gave the animals time to gain strength and become self-sustaining; it was healthy because the flesh of the animals was not wholesome to eat during the first week of life. Judaism taught that animals could not be offered to God until one sabbath had passed. Priests were not permitted to sacrifice a mother and its offspring on the same day (v. 28). Killing successive generations in one day was cruel and inhumane and not in keeping with the spirit of atonement, which is a portrayal of life being spared because a life has been vicariously sacrificed. The animals were to be freely offered (v. 29) and eaten on the same day of the sacrifice; nothing could remain for the next day (v. 30). Through the centuries, Israel failed miserably in following God's law by offering defiled sacrifices, thus polluting His altar (Mal. 1:7–14).

Believer-priests are to "offer up spiritual sacrifices, acceptable to God by Jesus Christ" (1 Pet. 2:5). This is the sacrifice of praise and thanksgiving continually given to the Lord, along with sharing what we have with others (Heb. 13:15–16). Our spiritual sacrifices are to be carried from the altars of our hearts in service for the Lord; any other type of worship or service is defiled and unacceptable to Him.

The priests were given four reasons why they were to keep the commandments set forth by God. First and preeminently, He had the rightful authority over them: "I am the Lord" (v. 31). Second, He planned to manifest His holiness through them as an example for all to see: "I will be hallowed among the children of Israel" (v. 32). Third, He purchased them to manifest His program through Himself: "Who brought you out of the land of Egypt" (v. 33). Fourth, the privilege of relationship should produce obedience: "to be your God" (v. 33).

These reasons hold true for believer-priests as well. God has rightful authority over them because of redemption, having planned that they should manifest His holiness to a lost world. Believer-priests, being brought into such a high privilege of relationship, must continually guard their commitment, lest they be disqualified from service because of sin. Peter stated it well: "But, as he who hath called you is holy, so be ye holy in all manner of life" (1 Pet. 1:15). We are not to *become* holy but to *be* holy in every relationship of life. This is not impossible in our day, for God, who has called us, also provides the spiritual power for holiness to all who avail themselves of it through the Holy Spirit.

William D. Longstaff gave the key to maintaining personal purity in character and conduct before the Lord in the hymn, "Take Time to Be Holy":

> Take time to be holy, The world rushes on;
>   Much time spend in secret with Jesus alone;
> By looking to Jesus, Like Him thou shalt be;
>   Thy friends in thy conduct His likeness shall see.

Seeing, then, that we have a great high priest, that is passed into the heavens, Jesus, the Son of God, let us hold fast our profession. For we have not an high priest who cannot be touched with the feeling of our infirmities, but was in all points tempted like as we are, yet without sin.

Hebrews 4:14–15

CHAPTER 20

Christ, The Superior Priest

(Hebrews 4:14–15)

T he high priest, clothed in the beautiful garments of his office, moved gracefully about the Tabernacle ministering on behalf of Israel. No one was held in higher esteem among the people than he. No one enjoyed greater privilege to experience the sweet fellowship of God's presence than he. No one held a more prominent position on earth than he. Yet, with all of his privilege, position, and prominence, he was not a perfect high priest; he was subject to infirmities and death like all men.

The Aaronic priesthood was only a shadow of the perfect priesthood of which Christ is the superior fulfiller—superior because He is of a more excellent order than Aaron; superior because He made a more excellent sacrifice; superior because He has a more excellent ministry and is still functioning on our behalf. In the chapters to follow, you will experience the majestic beauty of Christ's high priestly ministry as revealed in the Scriptures.

Christ is Superior in Selection

The high priest was selected "from among men" (v. 1) for the sole purpose of representing the people as their mediator before

God. He was not chosen by the people or self-appointed but was divinely "ordained" (v. 1) in his call. "And no man taketh this honor unto himself, but he that is called of God, as was Aaron" (v. 4).

Some, like Korah, Dathan, and Abiram, tried to challenge the divine ordination of Aaron's high priesthood, stating that he took too much authority upon himself as the only one to represent Israel before God (Num. 16:1–3). Moses accepted their challenge. He had Korah and his followers come before the Lord with censers full of incense and fire to determine whom the Lord had ordained. God vindicated Aaron's high priestly call when the ground opened and swallowed Korah and those who stood with him (Num. 16:32). God added further confirmation of Aaron as His choice by the miraculous budding of his rod (Num. 17).

Although Aaron's ordination was great, Christ's was greater. Aaron was only a man, but Christ is the God-Man, although He did not appoint or glorify Himself as high priest. God Himself ordained the Son into His eternal high priestly ministry.

Jesus is not only a high priest but a king-priest, which is clearly seen from two messianic Psalms. Christ's priesthood is anchored in His Sonship: "Thou art my Son, today have I begotten thee" (v. 5). This passage is taken from Psalm 2:7, which speaks of the kingly rule of the Lord after His resurrection.

He is a king-priest from a different order than that of Aaron: "Thou art a priest forever after the order of Melchizedek" (v. 6). This was prophesied in Psalm 110:4. First, Melchizedek was a king-priest, whereas Aaron was only a priest. No king dared enter the Temple to function as a priest without paying severe consequences. King Uzziah tried to minister in the priest's office and was stricken with leprosy until the day of his death (2 Chr. 26:16–21). But the Lord Jesus is both king and priest, ministering in both offices, because He is of a different order than Aaron. Second, Melchizedek stood alone, not having inherited his kingly priesthood or transmitting it to successors. But the Aaronic high priesthood was inherited and transmitted to many sons through the centuries. The Lord did not inherit or pass on His high priesthood. Third, Melchizedek had no recorded ending, typifying Christ, whose priesthood is eternal. Aaron, on the other hand, had to be replaced because of death. The Aaronic priesthood ceased with the destruction of Herod's Temple in 70 A.D.

Christ is Superior in Sympathy

The high priest was taken from among his brethren to represent the people before God. Like them, he suffered, being compassed with infirmity (weakness, v. 2). He, like his brethren, felt temptation, committed sins, would someday die, and had to give an account of his works before God. He understood those who sinned out of ignorance (Lev. 4) and those who wandered "out of the way" (v. 2), erring against God. Being conscious of his sin as well as the people's sin, he had compassion (lit., dealt gently) on the people whom he served.

In order for Christ to be a high priest, He could not take on the nature of an angel but had to take on the seed of Abraham and become a man like His brethren (Heb. 2:16–17), yet without sin. As a man, He knew the feelings and pains mortals face, but to a greater degree. He knew love and rejection, joy and sorrow, peace and fear. Physically, He experienced the natural sensations of a man, but even more so. He endured poverty and persecution and was forsaken by His friends when He needed them most; one even denied knowing Him before His death. Satan dogged Him throughout His life, trying to destroy Him whenever he had the opportunity—from birth to that last gasp on the cross. But the worst rejection occurred when, while hanging on the cross, God the Father deserted Him. No better words sum up His suffering than those of Isaiah: "He is despised and rejected of men, a man of sorrows, and acquainted with grief, and we hid as it were our faces from him; he was despised, and we esteemed him not" (Isa. 53:3).

The writer to the Hebrews drew back the curtain and gave us a glimpse of Jesus' agony before His death. Let us reverently enter the Garden of Gethsemane and witness it.

Falling prostrate on the ground, with the shadow of the cross looming up in His mind, He offered "prayers [beggings] and supplications with strong crying and tears unto

him that was able to save him from death" (v. 7). The mental
torment intensified with each moment, as His time drew
near. We see His pitiful pleading and uncontrollable sob-
bing, not to be saved "from death" that awaited Him but
"out of death" to be resurrected. He didn't shrink back from
the thought of dying, for He clearly predicted His own death
(Mt. 16:21; 17:22–23; 20:18–19). Nor should it be inferred that
He feared that the agony experienced in the garden would
cause His death. But He had foreseen the awful cup of
suffering that awaited Him and shrunk back in horror. In a
matter of hours, He would become a sin offering, separated
from God, bearing the sin of the whole world while hanging
on a cross. Yet never once did He seek His own will in the
matter, but only the Father's will. True, He said, "O my
Father, if it be possible, let this cup pass from me"; but He
also said, "nevertheless, not as I will, but as thou wilt" (Mt.
26:39). Jesus, the God-Man, humbled Himself in complete
dependence on His Father.

Through a life of suffering, Jesus "learned . . . obedience by the
things which he suffered" (v. 8). Naturally, He did not have to
learn obedience; He knew what it meant to obey. In fact, He said,
"I do always those things that please him [the Father]" (Jn. 8:29).
But it was necessary for Him to learn obedience, because the
growth experience was part of His humanity; He experienced all
the trials and temptations that people face in obedience to God.
To be a high priest who could feel with others, He had to experience life on a human level (Lk. 2:52).

Today, we can turn to a high priest who is greater than Aaron.
He is greater in His person because He is "the Son of God"
(Heb. 4:14); Aaron was only a man. His physical affliction was
greater because He went through more severe suffering than
Aaron, even the suffering of crucifixion (1 Pet. 2:23–24). His perfection was greater than Aaron's because He was tempted in all
areas of life that we experience, "yet without sin" (Heb. 4:15).
His position is greater because He passed through the heavens
to minister on our behalf (Heb. 4:14). His privilege is greater

because He is "seated on the right hand of the throne of the Majesty in the heavens" (Heb. 8:1); thus, He is able to sympathize with believers in any trials or temptations they face.

Because believers have such a great high priest who knows their weaknesses, feels with them in every situation, and knows what it is like to be tempted, they are bidden to come (Heb. 4:16)—come to God's throne, which, through Christ the high priest, is a place of grace (unmerited favor) and mercy. Believers are to come boldly (lit., in a spirit of freedom and frankness), bearing their hearts before God and letting Him know any weaknesses they possess (Heb. 4:16).

When believers come to Christ, the result is threefold. First, they find mercy because Christ understands their infirmities, having suffered in the flesh. Second, they find grace through Christ's suffering on the cross. He has opened the way for the loving God to provide redemption for sinners. Third, they find help in time of need. No matter how severe the difficulty, night or day, all year long, the throne of grace is open to provide help (Heb. 4:16). The Aaronic high priest was never able to provide such complete grace and mercy to those he served; but Christ, our high priest, is able.

Christ' ability to help in any need was a source of great encouragement and comfort to Hebrew Christians in the first century, who suffered severe trials because of their faith. Knowing that they had a great high priest, they were exhorted to cling tenaciously to their profession (lit., confession) of Christ (Heb. 4:14). In like manner, believers today are exhorted to continually uphold their testimony to a lost world, no matter what or how severe the opposition.

Christ is Superior in Sacrifice

The ministry of the high priest was to offer "gifts and sacrifices" for the sins of himself and those of the people (vv. 1, 3). These were not the various gifts and sacrifices offered on the sabbath or special feast days (Lev. 1—7), but those offered on the day of atonement, when the high priest entered the holy of holies to offer gifts (incense, Lev. 16:12) and animal sacrifices (Lev. 16).

The death of Christ was a priestly act. He did not offer gifts and sacrifices, but Himself as the spotless Lamb of God (1 Pet. 1:19) to atone for sin. He was both the priest offering the sacrifice (Heb. 8:3) and the sacrifice being offered (Heb. 9:14). Jesus, the high priest, purchased redemption for mankind through His own blood (Heb. 9:12) and did not have to offer sacrifices continually, as Aaron did. He appeared once to bear the sins of many, putting away sin by the sacrifice of Himself (Heb. 9:26, 28).

Through the suffering sacrifice of Himself, Jesus is "made perfect" (v. 9). Of course, He was not morally incomplete, but through His suffering and death on the cross, He was consecrated as a high priest, becoming a complete Savior and ushering in a completed salvation forevermore. He is the author (lit., principal cause)—not a temporary salvation, as was Aaron—of an "eternal salvation unto all them that obey him" (v. 9). Salvation is not bestowed universally to all people; it is given only to those who obey by putting their faith in Christ.

Through His suffering, obedience, and sacrifice, Jesus is fit to be "Called [designated or greeted] . . . an high priest after the order of Melchizedek" (v. 10). Like Melchizedek, Christ is a high priest "forever" (v. 6), and His ministry is permanent because He continually functions on behalf of believers.

Christ's ministry as a high priest is superior to Aaron's. Aaron only offered sacrifices; Christ offered a perfect sacrifice, once and for all. Aaron had to offer a sacrifice for his own sin; Christ was sinless. Aaron offered a sacrifice external to himself; Christ offered Himself. Aaron provided only a covering for sin; Christ secured an eternal salvation. Aaron's atonement was for Israel; Christ's atonement is for all people, although it is efficacious only for those who believe (Pink, *An Exposition of Hebrews, p. 258).

The writer to the Hebrews thrilled our hearts by presenting the superior high priesthood of the Lord. We eagerly hang on every word, wanting him to go deeper into Christ's holy and heavenly ministry. But he was reluctant to do so. The writer was not afraid that the subject was too difficult or that he lacked the skills to teach it. Rather, the difficulty was with his hearers. The first problem was their spiritual condition. His listeners were "dull of hearing" (slothful) [v. 11]. They had drifted away and become insensitive to deeper teaching regarding the priesthood of the Lord.

The second problem was their spiritual capacity. Although they had been believers for a long time, their Christian walk had degenerated. Slothfulness had caused stagnation, which was stunting their spiritual growth. They were not able to take the meat of the Word and had to be nursed on the milk concepts of Christ (v. 13). It became necessary for the writer to reteach his hearers the first principles (ABCs) of Christianity, which do not require great mental ability to digest. New babes in Christ are beautiful to behold, but they become grotesque if they remain babes after 30 years.

The third problem was their spiritual callousness. Dull, degenerate Christians are callous when discerning good and evil (v. 14). If believers do not exercise themselves in the study of God's Word, they will remain spiritual infants.

How does your spiritual report card read? If it does not say, "Student is attentive to God's Word, is able to assimilate and apply spiritual principles, is progressing well in spiritual growth," then you have some homework to do.

I trust you have given considerable thought to your relationship with the Lord. If not, why not do something about it? Talk it over with the Lord and allow Him to reign supreme on the throne of your life.

So also Christ glorified not himself to be made an high priest, but he that said unto him, Thou art my Son, today have I begotten thee. As he saith also in another place, Thou art a priest forever after the order of Melchizedek.

Hebrews 5:5–6

CHAPTER 21

Christ, The Sovereign Priest

(Hebrews 5; 7)

T he ministry of the priests was the focal point of Judaism. The priests were held in highest esteem among the people as the ones who represented them before God, made atonement for sin, and instructed them in righteousness. They tenaciously clung to the priests' ministry as their only hope of acceptance with God.

The Jews of the first century were faced with some perplexing questions concerning Christ's high priestly ministry. Why wasn't He called a priest during His earthly ministry? How could He be a legitimate high priest if He was not from the tribe of Levi? Because Christ was not from the tribe of Levi, was His atoning work efficacious on their behalf?

The writer to the Hebrews reached back into the Old Testament and, under the inspiration of the Holy Spirit, presented an obscure truth that had been hidden for two millennia. Christ was a high priest after the order of Melchizedek (Heb. 5:6, 10; 6:20), not after the priesthood of Aaron. Melchizedek? Yes, Melchizedek! He is one of the most significant types in Scripture to validate Christ's high priestly ministry.

Christ is a Preeminent High Priest

Much controversy has revolved around Melchizedek. He briefly stepped onto the stage of biblical history and then vanished. He was first mentioned in connection with Abraham soon after he delivered his nephew Lot from King Chedorlaomer and those with him in the valley of Shaveh (Gen. 14:17). But who was this Melchizedek?

His Priesthood

The writer to the Hebrews stated that he was "king of Salem, priest of the Most High God" (v. 1). This phrase reveals more than appears on the surface. His name means *king (melchi) of righteousness (zedek)*. He was from Salem, later known as Jerusalem, which means *peace*. He was priest of the Most High God (Heb., *El Elyon)*, which literally means *God the Highest*, speaking of the true and living God. His very name, place of residence, and ministry typify Christ as king-priest. Christ is the righteous one (1 Jn. 2:1) who secures peace (Eph. 2:14) for all people who put their faith in Him. Today, the Lord functions as high priest, sitting at the right hand of God (Heb. 8:1). He will not fulfill His kingly role until He comes as King of kings to sit on the throne of David (Lk. 1:31–33).

Little is known of Melchizedek's background. Hebrews simply says that he was "Without father, without mother, without descent [genealogy], having neither beginning of days nor end of life, but made like unto the Son of God, abideth a priest continually" (v. 3). Some interpret this verse to be a preincarnate appearance of Christ, similar to His appearance to Abraham (Gen. 18:1). This cannot be the case, however, because the text simply says that he is "made *like* the Son of God" (v. 3) and not that he *was* the son of God. Melchizedek was made like Christ; Christ was not made like Melchizedek. In the revelation of Melchizedek, God concealed the details of his life. Because his priesthood continues, not having a recorded genealogy or a beginning or end, he is a type of Christ.

His Prominences

To convince the Hebrew Christians that Melchizedek was of a greater priesthood than Aaron, the writer set forth a twofold contrast. First, Melchizedek was greater than Abraham.

1. Abraham, progenitor of the nation of Israel, acknowledged Melchizedek's superiority over him by giving him a tenth of the spoil taken from the five kings he defeated (vv. 2, 4; cp. Gen. 14:20).
2. Melchizedek was superior to Abraham because he existed before him, being without descent (genealogy) [v. 6].
3. Melchizedek was superior to Abraham in that he had no genealogical connection with Abraham or the Levitical priesthood, because Levi sprang from Abraham (v. 10).
4. Melchizedek was superior to Abraham in that the lesser was blessed by the greater (v. 7). Abraham, already blessed by God and having received great promises from Him (Gen. 12:1–3), in turn blessed Melchizedek. This made him greater than Abraham.

Second, the Melchizedekian priest was greater than the Aaronic priesthood.

1. Levi, who was a descendant of Abraham, had the right to receive tithes from the other 11 tribes, according to the Mosaic law (v. 5).
2. All of the Levitical priests who received tithes died, but there is no record of Melchizedek's death, thus, his priesthood stands as a living and continuing office (v. 8).
3. The Levitical priests who received tithes, although unborn, paid tithes to Melchizedek through their great-grandfather Abraham (vv. 9–10), thus, the lesser (Levi) paid tithes to the greater (Melchizedek).

This beautiful truth shows the greatness of the Lord Jesus' high priesthood. Melchizedek, the king-priest, was superior to the Aaronic priesthood. But, with all his greatness, Melchizedek was only a type of the true high priest, Jesus Christ, who is preeminent over all priests. Thus, Christ is the priest who can meet all the needs of Hebrew Christians, as well as all other Christians.

Christ is a Perfect High Priest

Not only was Melchizedek's priesthood superior to the Aaronic priesthood on historical grounds, but it was to replace it for theological reasons. The Aaronic priesthood fell short of perfection (v. 11) because it could not bring believers to a right or complete standing before God through the expiation of sins (not that believers become sinless). Neither could perfection be attained through the Mosaic law, which was inseparably linked to the Aaronic priesthood, for under it the people received the law (v. 11). Because the priesthood was to be changed, the law had to be changed as well (v. 12). If the priesthood did not stand, neither would the law, which had been given in connection with the priesthood.

The law, being "holy, and just, and good" (Rom. 7:12), demanded perfect righteousness, which sinful men, functioning in the office of priest, could not provide. Therefore, mankind's hope for a perfect standing before God had to be brought about outside the Aaronic priesthood and the Mosaic law. Christ is the only one qualified to function as high priest on behalf of sinful mankind (Rom. 8:3).

This was a new concept to Hebrew Christians in the first century, and many found it difficult to understand and accept. Their faith had been centered in the Aaronic priesthood and the Mosaic law, which were the embodiment of Judaism for centuries. Yet Jesus had stated that the new faith could not be poured into old wineskins or used as a patch to strengthen their Jewish beliefs (Mk. 2:21–22).

The writer then gave a number of reasons why Christ's priesthood, after the order of Melchizedek, supersedes the Aaronic priesthood in perfection. First, Christ was not from the tribe of Levi but from another tribe (v. 13). The Lord "sprang out of Judah, " from David's seed (Isa. 11:1; Mt. 1:1; Acts 2:29–31; Rom. 1:3), and Moses never spoke of a priesthood from the tribe of Judah (v. 14). God graciously planned and predicted this development centuries before it occurred.

Second, the Aaronic priesthood was after the "carnal [fleshly] commandment" (v. 16), such as Aaronic descent, offering animal sacrifices, and following priestly regulations stipulated in the law of Moses. But Christ's priesthood was "after the power of an endless [indissoluble] life" (v. 16). He is the eternal Son of God (Jn. 1:1), creator and sustainer of all things (Col. 1:16–17), the

"Alpha and Omega" (Rev. 1:8), has power over life (Jn. 10:15–18), and, unlike the Aaronic priest, has power to bestow eternal life (Jn. 11:25–26). Christ's indissoluble priesthood was prophesied long before His birth when David wrote, "Thou art a priest forever after the order of Melchizedek" (Ps. 110:4; Heb. 7:17).

Because the Aaronic priesthood is no longer in effect, there is "an annulling of the commandment" (v. 18). There are three reasons for this annulling of the law.

1. The priesthood, being changed, necessitated a change of the law (v. 12).
2. The law, although holy, just, and good, was weak and unprofitable (v. 18) in that it could never provide or produce righteousness in mankind. Paul stated that "the law was our schoolmaster to bring us unto Christ, that we might be justified by faith" (Gal. 3:24). The law was added because of sin, "till the seed [Christ] should come" (Gal. 3:19), limiting mankind to justification by faith as the only way to be declared righteous before God (Gal. 3:23).
3. "The law made nothing perfect [complete]" (v. 19), for it could not bring mankind into a right standing before God. It was only temporary (Gal. 3:19) and "a shadow of good things to come" (Heb. 10:1). But "Christ is the end of the law for righteousness" (Rom. 10:4).

In fact, the law never did bring people "near unto God" (v. 19); it kept them far from God. Although the law has been annulled, it did pave the way for a "better hope" (v. 19) through the priesthood of Christ, who could bring people to a perfect (right) standing before God.

Third, Christ was ordained to His priesthood by an eternal oath after the order of Melchizedek (vv. 20–21), but the Aaronic priesthood was not. Thus, being made a priest by an oath, Jesus is the "surety" (guarantee) that God will keep the promises He made to believers in the New Covenant, which He inaugurated through His shed blood (v. 22).

Fourth, the Aaronic priesthood was temporary; its priests had to be replaced because of death (v. 23). In contrast, Christ's priesthood is "unchangeable," meaning it was inviolable and untransmittable because He continues to live forever (v. 24). Christ's priesthood was incapable of being altered or passed on to a successor.

Because Christ is an unchangeable high priest, "he is able also to save them to the uttermost that come unto God by him" (v. 25). This verse is not speaking of God's ability to save people out of the depths of sin, although He can. The word *uttermost* speaks of the *comprehensiveness* or *completeness* of our salvation. Christ saves the total person (body, soul, and spirit) from the power and penalty of sin and someday will deliver us from the presence of sin at our glorification. He is able to provide such complete salvation because "he ever liveth to make intercession for them" (v. 25). The word *intercession* encompasses Christ's entire ministry on behalf of believers, which is based on the merits of His sacrifice. He is an ever-living priest who continually intervenes in heaven before the throne of God for the needs of all believers.

In type, the Aaronic priesthood did the same thing for Israel. When the high priest entered the presence of God, he wore the name of each tribe on his breastplate, representing them before God. But Christ's priesthood is perfect, far exceeding the intercessory ministry of Aaron's priesthood.

Christ is a Pure High Priest

Having described the greatness of Christ's high priesthood, the writer to the Hebrews culminated his argument, almost shouting out, "such an high priest was fitting for us" (v. 26)! Because of His character, Christ is the only high priest suitable to officiate before God on behalf of sinful mankind. In simplistic beauty, the writer pulled together the salient features that he had already presented, painting a final portrait of Christ's great priesthood.

A Portrait of His Person

Christ is holy. There are two Greek words for *holy*. One *is hagios,* referring to people being *set apart to God by virtue of their standing,* like the Aaronic priests. The other word is *hosios,* which speaks of *holiness of character, an innate purity.* It is in this sense that Christ is holy. He is harmless (guileless). Christ is free from malice or deceit of any kind. He is undefiled, free from any moral impurity. He is separate from sinners. Christ associated with sinners, for He ate and drank with them, but He never sinned. He is made higher than the heavens. Christ has entered into the presence of God, being enthroned in the highest place of honor and power. His character makes Him a fitting high priest to meet mankind's needs!

A Portrait of His Provision

The Aaronic priesthood had to offer repeated sacrifices daily, because the blood of bulls and goats could not take away sin (Heb. 10:4). In contrast, Christ did not have to offer a sacrifice for His own sins, for He is sinless. Yet, for the sins of mankind He offered Himself once (lit., once for all) as a blood sacrifice to expiate sin. His sacrifice makes Him a fitting high priest to meet mankind's needs.

A Portrait of His Perpetualness

To persuade the Hebrew Christians of Christ's sovereign priesthood, the writer pulled together the threads of all that he had previously stated, showing a contrast between the two priesthoods. The Aaronic priests were ordained during the time of the law, but Christ's perfect priesthood is "since the law" (cp. Ps. 110:4), showing that He superseded them. They were ordained priests by the law, but Christ was ordained by "the word of the oath." They had infirmity (weakness of the flesh), but Christ is perfect. They were priests only during their lifetime, but Christ is a priest "for evermore" (Pink, *An Exposition of Hebrews*, p. 423). Christ's consecration as high priest is perfect and permanent in every detail and will continue eternally.

Oh, Christian friend, we can shout as well because "We have such an high priest" (Heb. 8:1)—an unchangeable priest who once for all offered Himself as a sacrifice for sins; a priest who is able to save to the uttermost, seated at the throne of God making intercession on our behalf; an ever-living priest whom we will someday see face to face and enjoy throughout eternity. With Peter we exclaim, "Lord, to whom shall we go? Thou hast the words of eternal life" (Jn. 6:68).

Now of the things which we have spoken this is the sum: We have such an high priest, who is seated on the right hand of the throne of the Majesty in the heavens . . . But now hath he obtained a more excellent ministry, by how much also he is the mediator of a better covenant, which was established upon better promises.

Hebrews 8:1, 6

CHAPTER 22

Covenant of the Savior

(Hebrews 8; 9:15–20)

The streets of Jerusalem were deserted. A quiet hush had fallen over the city that, on other days, was bustling with activity. Families had gathered in their homes to commemorate the Passover. In a large upper room, Jesus had assembled with His disciples to partake of the feast. Near the end of the service, He took a cup from the table, lifted it up for all to see, and said, "this is my blood of the new testament [covenant], which is shed for many for the remission of sins" (Mt. 26:28).

Most likely His disciples were surprised and puzzled by His statement. Questions may have flooded their minds: What did He mean when He said the cup represented His blood of a new covenant? How could Jesus' blood have anything to do with a covenant? What new covenant was He speaking about? Just how much the disciples understood of the prophetic pronouncement flowing from Jesus' lips is uncertain. But in a few short days, it all became clear as Jesus' statement changed their lives. In a short time, with marching orders in hand, they proclaimed this new covenant in all of Jerusalem, Judea, Samaria, and unto the uttermost part of the earth.

In preceding chapters, the credentials of Christ were presented, showing His superior priesthood. The succeeding chapters will focus on Christ's ministry as high priest, beginning with His mediatory work in establishing the New Covenant.

The Covenant Proclaimed

Although the Aaronic ministry was excellent, having been established by God, Christ has "obtained a more excellent ministry" (8:6). It is more excellent in nature for four reasons. First, Jesus is the Son of God, the eternal high priest, seated on the right hand of God (8:1). Second, He serves in the true heavenly sanctuary (8:2), whereas the Aaronic priests served in the earthly Tabernacle. Third, "he is the mediator of a better covenant, which was established upon better promises" (8:6). Fourth, the promises in the first covenant were conditional, earthly, fleshly, and temporary; but the New Covenant promises are unconditional, spiritual, and eternal.

The Covenant Promised

The New Covenant is contrasted with the "first covenant" (Mosaic Covenant) [8:7]. God entered into the Mosaic Covenant with the nation of Israel at Mount Sinai (Ex. 19:5; 34:27–28). This was not the first covenant God made with mankind, but it was the first one He made with Israel nationally.

The Mosaic Covenant did not alter, annul, or abrogate the provisions of the Abrahamic Covenant, for it was given 430 years after it (Gal. 3:17–19). Moses was careful to make the distinction between these two covenants (Dt. 5:2–3).

The Mosaic Covenant encompassed three areas of Israel's life: moral laws, which were spelled out in the Ten Commandments (Ex. 20:1–17); social laws, which were given to govern their relationships within the nation (Ex. 21:1–24: 11); and religious laws, which were provided to direct them in their worship of God (Ex. 24:12—31:18). But these Mosaic promises of blessing were conditional. The requisite was that Israel had to obey the commandments in order for God to fulfill His covenant promises to them, for He said, "if ye will obey my voice indeed, and keep my covenant, then ye shall be a peculiar treasure unto me above all people" (Ex. 19:5).

Israel failed to keep the covenant promises. The fault was not with the law, for the commandments were holy, just, and good (Rom. 7:12). The fault was not with with God, for He had taken "them by the hand to lead them out of the land of Egypt" (8:9) and cared for them throughout their wilderness journey (Dt. 1:30–31; 32:1–14). The fault was with mankind's sinful nature, which rebelled against the conditions stipulated in the covenant (8:8–9; Rom. 8:3), and the covenant itself was limited in power to provide spiritual life and righteousness for sinful mankind (8:7; Gal. 3:19–25). This is the same argument used to show that the Levitical priesthood had to be replaced (Heb. 7:11).

The Covenant Parties

Many views have been presented concerning the parties with whom God made the covenant. Some believe that God made two New Covenants, one with Israel and another with the church, but nowhere in the New Testament are two New Covenants mentioned.

Some believe that the New Covenant was made with Israel but applies to the church as well; thus, there is one covenant but two applications, one for the church now and another for Israel in the future. But the church cannot be fulfilling any of the provisions of Israel's New Covenant today because the covenant is made only with Israel and Judah, not with the church; the church has never been called Israel or a spiritual Israel in Scripture; and the covenant is to take affect in Israel after Christ's return, which precludes the church.

Some believe that God made only one New Covenant with Israel, ratified by Christ's blood, thus opening the way for Him to spiritually bless Jewish and Gentile believers during the church age. But the national, spiritual, and material provisions promised in the New Covenant will be fulfilled to Israel during the Millennium. This view seems more plausible.

But if the covenant was not made with the church, why was it presented in Hebrews 8? The writer quoted it to point out the failure of the Mosaic Covenant and to show Israel that a better covenant with better promises is to be anticipated in the future.

The New Covenant was instituted at the Lord's death (9:16–17), and the disciples ministered its concepts to the nation of Israel (2 Cor. 3:6). Because Israel rejected its Messiah nationally, the covenant was postponed, to be realized in its fullness when Christ returns to set up the Kingdom.

The Covenant Provisions

God realized the inability of the first covenant and announced its replacement through the Prophet Jeremiah six centuries before Christ. He said, "Behold, the days come, saith the Lord, when I will make a new covenant with the house of Israel and with the house of Judah" (8:8; cp. Jer. 31:31). What does this new covenant provide for Israel?

Israel's Renewed Relationship

God said, "I will be to them a God, and they shall be to me a people" (v. 10; cp. Jer. 31:33). This was the relationship Israel enjoyed under the first covenant, when God brought them out of Egypt and called the nation "my son" (Ex. 4:22). But Israel broke the relationship through spiritual infidelity (Ezek. 16; Hos. 1:9), causing God to discipline them through judgment.

God has never ceased to love Israel. He prefaced the giving of the New Covenant with the words, "Yea, I have loved thee with an everlasting love; therefore, with loving-kindness have I drawn thee" (Jer. 31:3). This verse was uttered after God had described, in vivid language, the deplorable situation of Israel (Jer. 30:12–14). In the New Covenant, God is "merciful to their unrighteousness" (v. 12) and has renewed His relationship with them.

The New Covenant, unlike the Mosaic Covenant, is unconditional. Six times in the covenant God said, "I will" (vv. 8, 10, 12), meaning that He will fulfill the provisions of the covenant. Its fulfillment depends solely on the integrity of God, not on the faithfulness of Israel.

Israel's Regeneration

The New Covenant provides an inner change of mind and heart that can be produced only through regeneration. God said, "I will put my laws into their mind, and write them in their hearts" (v. 10; cp. Jer. 31:33).

The first covenant was external, engraved in stone (Ex. 32:15–16; 2 Cor. 3:7). God promised to bless the people, conditioned on their obedience, but the people failed. The New Covenant is written "in fleshy tables of the heart" (2 Cor. 3:3) through the Holy Spirit's ministry. This spiritual birth will take place at Christ's Second Coming, when God will pour out His Spirit on Israel, bringing about their repentance from sin and acceptance of Jesus as their Messiah (Zech. 12:10; Rom. 11:26). Israel will be born in a day (Isa. 66:8).

With a new heart (Jer. 24:7; Ezek. 36:26), no one in Israel will have to have his neighbor (fellow citizen) teach him about the Lord, for all will know Him, "from the least to the greatest" (v. 11; cp. Jer. 31:34). The first covenant provided for only the religious leaders to be taught the legal concepts of the law with its complicated rituals and regulations. In the Kingdom, believers will not need a priest to teach them, for the Lord will teach them (Isa. 54:13; Jn. 6:45) through the indwelling Holy Spirit. They will be empowered to walk in the way of the Lord and keep His statutes and ordinances (Ezek. 36:27).

Regeneration provides forgiveness of sin. The Lord said, "I will be merciful to their unrighteousness, and their sins and their iniquities will I remember no more" (v. 12; cp. Jer. 31:34). Under the first covenant, there was a continual remembrance of sin each time an animal sacrifice was offered (Heb. 10:3). These animal sacrifices never took away sin; they only covered them (Heb. 10:4). Jesus was the sacrificial lamb (Jn. 1:29) who, once and for all, took away sin (Heb. 10:15–18) through His blood of the New Covenant. Strong assurance that God had forgiven Israel's sins was presented through the use of a double negative, "no more," meaning *no, never, not under any condition* will He remember their sins. It was prophesied that "the blood of thy covenant" would procure these blessings for Israel in the Kingdom (Zech. 9:11).

Israel's Reconciler (9:15–20)

Christ is the mediator of the New Covenant (v. 15). A mediator acts as a middleman or go-between to intervene between two parties of differing backgrounds who desire to come into covenant relationship. A mediator must set aside his own interests for those of the parties involved in the mediation. He must be trustworthy and acceptable to the parties involved in the covenant. He must be able to secure a covenant for the parties involved through proper mediation. Through death, Christ is the mediator of the New Covenant, and He has made reconciliation possible to all who put their trust in His atoning work on their behalf. His mediatorship reaches back to the called ones under the first covenant (v. 15), as well as to those who will believe in the future.

Christ bestows an "eternal inheritance" (v. 15) on all believers through the New Covenant. The writer to the Hebrews gave a vivid illustration of this point through a description of the disposition of property in a legal will. An inheritance that has been bequeathed can be legally acquired only upon the death of the bequeather (v. 16). For the New Covenant to take effect and legally bestow salvation to sinners, Christ had to die (v. 17).

Even the Mosaic Covenant had to be inaugurated with blood to be effective (v. 18). Moses mediated the first covenant by taking the book of the covenant, reading it before the people, who agreed to keep its precepts (Ex. 24:7), and then sprinkling both the book and the people with blood (vv. 19–20).

The first covenant, being dedicated with blood, shows that the sacrificial death of an innocent victim was required to consecrate and establish the covenant. The Abrahamic Covenant was consecrated with blood (Gen. 15:7–17). These were only types and shadows, looking forward to the day when Christ will consecrate and establish a New Covenant through His shed blood (Mt. 26:28). He is the only one who can mediate the New Covenant between God and mankind (1 Tim. 2:5).

The Covenant's Permanence

The New Covenant, unlike the Mosaic Covenant, is eternal. The Lord said, "I will make a covenant of peace with them; it shall be an everlasting covenant with them" (Ezek. 37:26). What, then, happened to the Mosaic Covenant? Having served its purpose, it became inoperative. The words *old, decayeth,* and *groweth old* (8:13) show that the Mosaic Covenant was worn out, antiquated, and waning in strength, soon to be dissolved. But the Mosaic Covenant, although inoperative because of the New Covenant established by Christ, was still kept by Judah. Its ritualistic sacrifices and priestly regulations were maintained until Rome destroyed the Temple and dissolved the priesthood in 70 A.D. Even today, some 19 centuries, later Orthodox Judaism zealously clings to the Mosaic law. It must be asked of those who look to the Mosaic Covenant as a way to please God, Where is your priesthood to mediate the covenant promises? Where is your Temple to offer sacrifices for sin? Where is your holy of holies to offer atoning blood on Yom Kippur, the day of atonement? Naturally, they have all been dissolved. Why, then, do people cling so tenaciously to the Mosaic law, which cannot provide spiritual life or forgiveness of sin? They must come to Jesus who, as high priest, mediates a better covenant with better promises.

Christians have been given the great privilege of enjoying the spiritual blessings of the New Covenant mediated through the Messiah, a privilege for which they should be eternally thankful. But with privilege comes responsibility—responsibility to share the New Covenant blessings with others. Remember, someone did that for you!

But Christ being come an high priest of good things to come, by a greater and more perfect tabernacle, not made with hands, that is to say, not of this building, Neither by the blood of goats and calves, but by his own blood he entered in once into the holy place, having obtained eternal redemption for us.

Hebrews 9:11–12

CHAPTER 23

Christ, The Serving Priest

(Hebrews 9)

T he Tabernacle stood in simplistic beauty, a pillar of smoke resting on it by day and a pillar of fire by night, symbolizing the presence of God. So significant was this small building that 50 chapters of Scripture were devoted to revealing its structure and service. On seven occasions, the Tabernacle is described as being made according to a heavenly pattern. When referring to the heavenly sanctuary and its worship, the writer to the Hebrews did not speak of the Solomonic or Herodian Temples; instead, he went back to the Tabernacle, which, with its sacrifices and service, originally typified the Lord's ministry in heaven. But the Tabernacle was only a shadow of the real sanctuary in heaven. The writer then ascended the heights of heaven, taking us out of the shadows to reveal in great detail the superior ministry of Christ in the heavenly sanctuary.

The Hebrew Sanctuary

The Sanctuary

The first (Mosaic) covenant had laws governing the "divine service, and an earthly sanctuary" (v. 1) used by the priests to intercede on behalf of the people. The sanctuary consisted of two rooms. "The first was the [holy place], in which was the lamp-stand, and the table, and the showbread" (v. 2). The "golden censer" (golden altar) [v. 4] is depicted in the holy of holies, but it was actually in the holy place. The writer was referring to the ritual use of the altar, in which the high priest took the golden censer filled with burning incense into the holy of holies on the day of atonement (Lev. 16:12–13).

The second section of the sanctuary was called "the Holiest of all" (holy of holies) and had a huge "second veil" (v. 3) covering its entrance. The holy of holies contained only "the ark of the covenant overlaid round about with gold, in which was the golden pot that had manna, and Aaron's rod that budded, and the tables of the covenant" (v. 4). Two pure gold "cherubim" (v. 5) stood on the lid of the ark (mercy seat) facing each other but looking down toward the mercy seat with their wings touching as they stretched out over its top. The writer, after describing the Tabernacle and its furnishings, passed over their fulfillment in Christ, because the Tabernacle was only a type and shadow of Christ's earthly ministry, which was already completed. He focused instead on Christ's ministry in the heavenly sanctuary.

The Sanctuary Service

Priests ministered in "the first tabernacle" (holy place) [v. 6] daily. They trimmed and lit the golden lampstand, partook of and changed the showbread, and burned sweet incense (repre-senting the prayers of Israel to God) morning and evening on the golden altar of incense.

The high priest entered the second room (holy of holies) only "once every year, not without blood" (v. 7). This was on the day of atonement (Yom Kippur), the tenth day of Tishri (September-October). The high priest, divested of his royal dress and clothed in white linen (Lev. 16:4), parted the huge veil and entered the holy of holies to offer blood "for himself, and for the errors [sins of ignorance] of the people" (v. 7). It was necessary that he enter to offer blood, for "without shedding of blood is no remission" of sin (v. 22; cp. Lev. 17:11). This was a day either of judgment or of life for the people—judgment, for if the Lord did not accept the blood atonement, the high priest would die in the holy of holies, and the people would not have their sins covered; life, for if the high priest emerged alive, God had accepted the blood atonement for sin.

The Tabernacle and its regulations had been given by direct revelation from God, but it was only a "figure [lit., parable] for the time then present" (v. 9). A parable is an earthly story used to illustrate or teach a spiritual truth. The ordered service of the Tabernacle, mediated through the Levitical priesthood, was used as an object lesson in which the "Holy Spirit" (v. 8) taught the true realities of God to Israel.

First, the Spirit taught "that the way into the holiest of all was not yet made manifest, while the first tabernacle was yet standing" (v. 8). In other words, the way into the holy of holies was not disclosed until the inner veil between the two rooms was rent at Christ's crucifixion. At that time, all people had access through Christ into God's presence. Opening the holy of holies was an indication to the Levitical priesthood that their ministry had been dissolved.

Second, the Spirit taught that the Israelites could not be made perfect (brought into a right relationship with God) by means of the gifts and sacrifices they offered (v. 9). The sacrifices were powerless to take away sin; thus, the worshipers experienced no peace but had a guilty conscience (v. 9).

Third, the Spirit taught that such ordinances as "foods and drinks, and various washings" were "carnal" (fleshly) [v. 10]. The word *carnal* does not mean *sinful*; rather, it indicates that these sacrificial and ceremonial regulations were impotent to bring the Israelites into a right standing before God.

The sacrificial system was imposed on Israel "until the time of reformation" (lit., setting things right, a complete rectification) [v. 10]. The Tabernacle and its service were a shadow, figure, and parable pointing to a new and better program that God would establish through the ministry of Christ. The day of rectification came when the veil was rent so that people could come directly to God through the blood of Christ. This is what God had designed under the first covenant (Gal. 3:23–24).

The Heavenly Sanctuary

With the words, "But Christ being come an high priest" (v. 11), the writer presented a contrast between the old ministry under the Mosaic Covenant and the new ministry under Christ. Now the focus was on His heavenly ministry as "high priest of good things to come" (v. 11), in which the law was only a shadowy outline (10:1). He then enumerated a number of good things that Christ provided for believers.

Christ is in a better sanctuary. His ministry is in a "greater and more perfect tabernacle, not made with hands . . . not of this building" (creation) [v. 11]. He did not enter into a physical sanctuary made of earthly materials visible to the eye, but into heaven itself to dwell at the right hand of God. He is "minister of the sanctuary, and of the true tabernacle, which the Lord pitched, and not man" (8:2).

Christ is a better sacrifice. He entered the holy place, the heavenly sanctuary, not "by the blood of goats and calves, but by his own blood" (v. 12). Did Christ present His blood in heaven? The text does not say he entered in "with" His blood but "by" His blood—by virtue of His atoning work at the time of His death. He entered into the heavenly sanctuary not with literal blood, but with the *blood-right* atonement for mankind's sins. Unlike the Levitical high priest, who entered each year to offer blood, Christ entered once, there to remain as the advocate for believers.

Christ's sacrifice is better in sufficiency. His sacrifice was sufficient to obtain "eternal redemption" (v. 12). The words *for us* are in italics in the text, indicating that they were added by the translator for clarity. The emphasis of the verse is not on "eternal redemption *for us*" but on His entering in once and for all to secure eternal redemption, which is available to everyone but is only effectual for those who willingly receive Christ.

Christ's sacrifice secures a better sanctification. Any priest who touched a dead body or tomb was considered ceremonially unclean and could not enter the Tabernacle for service. The word *unclean* refers to being *unhallowed* or *profane* and thus unfit for service. Priests could be brought back into fellowship only through "the blood of bulls and of goats, and the ashes of an heifer sprinkling the unclean" (v. 13; cp. Lev. 16:3, 14–15; Num. 19:9–17). The blood of animals sanctified only "to the purifying of the flesh" (v. 13), which restored the priests to external purity, making them fit to serve.

The phrase "How much more shall the blood of Christ" (v. 14) shows the superiority of Christ's service over that of animal blood in a number of ways.

1. If the blood of animals provided external sanctification, how much more shall the blood of Christ provide internal cleansing from sin's defilement?
2. If the blood of insensible and involuntary animals could cleanse the flesh from defilement, how much more shall Christ (who through the eternal Spirit voluntarily shed His blood) cleanse from sin's defilement?
3. If beasts without merit, although considered perfect in body, could provide external cleansing, how much more could Christ (who offered himself without spot to God) cleanse from sin?
4. If the blood of animals purged the Israelites from ceremonial defilement, how much more did Christ's blood purge their conscience from dead works to serve the living God? No matter how meticulously the Levitical priests performed their service, they always felt a sense of guilt and defilement, but in Christ believers are liberated to experience perfect peace.

Christ's sacrifice has a better scope. Through His blood, Christ became the mediator of the New Covenant, securing an "eternal inheritance" (v. 15) for all believers. The scope of His mediatorship reaches back to include all the called ones (v. 15) under the first covenant, as well as those who will believe in the future. The inheritance bequeathed can be acquired only upon the death of the bequeather (v. 16). Thus, the new covenant can legally take effect only upon the death of Christ (v. 17).

To prove the necessity of a blood atonement, the writer to the Hebrews illustrated that even the first covenant did not become effective until Moses read it before the people, who agreed to keep its precepts (Ex. 24:7). Then Moses sprinkled the covenant, people, Tabernacle, and vessels of ministry with blood and water

(vv. 18–21). There are no exceptions when it comes to the necessity of cleansing mankind through a blood atonement, for "without shedding of blood is no remission" (v. 22). God takes the sin question seriously: No shed blood, no remission of sin!

The Heavenly Service

The mediatorial ministry of Christ's high priesthood reaches its culmination in the heavenly holy of holies. The earthly Tabernacle had to be "purified with these" (animal sacrifices) [v. 23] because of the defiling presence of the high priest (Lev. 16:6). In the same manner, the heavenly sanctuary must be cleansed "with better sacrifices" (v. 23)—Christ's sacrifice.

Scripture gives a number of reasons why the heavenly things, which are perfect, must be purified. First, the blood does not remove defilement from the sanctuary but prepares the sanctuary so that sinful people can serve there without defiling it. Second, Satan had access to heaven (Job 1:6; Rev. 12:9–10); thus, it had to be purified because of his presence. Third, the account of the unsaved is recorded in books kept in heaven (Rev. 20:12). Heaven must be cleansed of all things that speak of sin.

Christ's mediatorial ministry accrues a number of benefits to believers that are expressed and contrasted with those of the Levitical priesthood. The three appearances mentioned in these verses correspond to those of the high priest on the day of atonement.

Christ's Past Appearance

The word *appeared* (Gr., *phanerao*) [v. 26] means *has been manifested*, referring to His manifestation on earth to put away sin. The Levitical high priest "entereth into the holy place every year with the blood of others" (not his own) [v. 25] to make atonement. The Levitical priests had to repeat their yearly offering of blood, but not so with Christ, who entered into the heavenly sanctuary once, not offering "himself often, as the high priest" (v. 25). Why? "For then must he often have suffered since the foundation of the world" (v. 26). Because blood has always been required to atone for sin, Christ would have been obligated to repeatedly offer Himself as a suffering sacrifice to atone for sin in each generation, and that would have been impossible! "But now once [once for all], in the end [consummation] of the ages, hath he appeared to put away sin by the sacrifice of himself" (v. 26). Christ came to earth as a sacrifice for sin when the past ages had reached their goal in God's program (Gal. 4:4–5).

Another comparison, the death of mankind, was presented to show that Christ's offering of Himself cannot be repeated: "And as it is appointed unto men once to die, but after this the judgment, So Christ was once offered to bear the sins of many" (vv. 27–28). The thrust of this passage is the one-time offering of Christ for sin. If people are required to die only once, followed by judgment because of sin, then Christ is required to die only once, in a nonrepeatable act, to atone for mankind's sin (cp. Rom. 5:12–21). From this comparison springs a sobering thought: Death places people into either heaven or hell. Those who are lost have only the Great White Throne Judgment awaiting them (Rev. 20:11–15).

Christ's Present Appearance

The Levitical high priest "entered into the holy places made with hands," which were only patterns (corresponding copies) of the true sanctuary in heaven, to represent Israel before God on the day of atonement. Christ entered into heaven itself (before God's throne) to function as the believers' high priest. The phrase "now to appear in the presence of God for us" is full of meaning. "Now," from that point on, Christ became the believers' high priest in the heavenly holy of holies. The word *appear* (Gr., *prosopo*) means *to be manifested* and speaks of Christ's presenting Himself as the believers' representative before the Father, having finished His earthly ministry. Christ is "in the presence of God" (lit., face to face with, nothing obscuring or intervening between Him and the Father). He is manifested face to face before God "for us." When Christ was accepted into fellowship with God the Father, all believers were included as well—a hard concept for the finite mind to grasp.

Christ's Promised Appearance

On the day of atonement, Aaron disappeared behind the veil to offer blood on the mercy seat as an atonement for sin. In the meantime, the Israelites waited, looking expectantly for his return from the holy of holies to bless them. Those who have accepted Jesus Christ look (wait expectantly) for His return and blessing. Their expectation is not for naught, because He will "appear the second time." The word *appear* (Gr., *optomai*) means *to see* and has the idea of Christ's revealing Himself to the world at the Second Coming, at which time the promise made to His disciples in Acts 1:11 will be fulfilled. Christ's Second Coming will be "without [apart from] sin unto salvation." When Christ came the first time, He put away or settled the sin question by the sacrifice of Himself once for all. When He returns the second time, He will complete the salvation of the believers who will be alive on the earth at that time; the whole creation awaits this deliverance (Rom. 8:10–25).

Believers look with expectant joy for the Lord's return. Soon He will step out of the heavenly sanctuary and call His church home to glory. Those who have a part in the first resurrection will return as priests of God and Christ to reign with Him for a thousand years on the earth (Rev. 20:6). John W. Peterson summed up the believers' hope when he wrote,

Coming again, Coming again;
    Maybe morning, maybe noon,
Maybe evening and maybe soon!
    Coming again, Coming again;
O what a wonderful day it will be—
    Jesus is coming again!

And every priest standeth daily ministering and offering often the same sacrifices, which can never take away sins; But this man, after he had offered one sacrifice for sins forever, sat down on the right hand of God. . . For by one offering he hath perfected forever them that are sanctified.

Hebrews 10:11–12, 14

CHAPTER 24

Christ, The Superior Sacrifice
(Hebrews 10:1–31)

The sun was rising over the Mount of Olives, casting its golden glow on the Temple altar, as priests busied themselves preparing for the morning sacrifice. A priest, standing on the roof of a Temple building, announced that the first ray of light had reached Hebron. With the arrival of dawn, the priest cried out, "Priests, prepare for service, and Levites, for song!"

The sacrificial lamb had been examined thoroughly the night before, but it was reexamined just before being offered. Few worshipers witnessed the slaying of the lamb that took place with the opening of the great Temple gate. A priest, with a razor-sharp knife, made one quick cut to the throat of the lamb, causing instant death. Another priest caught the sacrificial blood in a golden bowl to be sprinkled on the altar. The offering of the morning sacrifice officially began the day of worship in the Temple.

Hundreds of Jewish people streamed into the Temple, weighted down with their offerings and sins. Rich men came with their costly sacrifices, while poor men tightly gripped pigeons or turtledoves. Daily the priests stood according to their chosen order, receiving the sacrifices of the people, uttering the proper prayers, then quickly slaying and preparing the offerings for the altar. Day after day, year after year, they followed the prescribed order set forth in the law, hoping that God would accept the offerings to atone for their sins. There had to be a superior sacrifice that would once and for all remove the people's sins; only God could provide such a sacrifice.

The Sacrifice Offered

The Mosaic law with its sacrificial system was only "a shadow [outline] of good things to come and not the very image [perfect likeness] of the things" (v. 1). In other words, the Mosaic system pointed out the need of and way to forgiveness, but it was at best an indefinite, dark outline and did not provide a true detailed picture of the sacrifice God would provide through Christ. These sacrifices, offered year after year, could never make the worshipers perfect (righteous in their standing before God) [v. 1].

The inability of the sacrifices to take away sin is illustrated in two ways. First, if the worshipers had been perfected by one sacrificial offering, it would have been needless to repeat the offering for sin. "For then would they not have ceased to be offered?" (v. 2). For example, if I break the law, I must pay the penalty. But once the penalty is paid, there is no need to continually pay it.

Second, if the Israelites had really been purged (having once been cleansed and kept clean) from their sins through their sacrifices, there would have been "no more consciousness [sense] of sins" (v. 2). But the "gifts and sacrifices . . .could not make him that did the service perfect, as pertaining to the conscience" (9:9). Therefore, the Israelites never felt free from the condemnation of past sins. In fact, "there is a remembrance again made of sins every year" (v. 3). On Yom Kippur (the day of atonement), sacrifices were offered, bringing to remembrance (calling to mind) the sins that the Israelites had committed. Yet in their hearts they knew that these sacrifices could not remove sin. The repetitious offering of the Levitical sacrifices proved their inability to cleanse from sin.

An interesting contrast can be made with the word *remembrance*. In the Lord's supper, Christ said, "this do . . . in remembrance of me" (1 Cor. 11:25). Every time believers partake of the Lord's supper, they remember that Christ has removed their sins forever through His sacrificial death.

Israel's sins were not removed because "it is not possible that the blood of bulls and of goats should take away sins" (v. 4). The blood of animals had no power to provide redemption; the ritual slayings could only purify the flesh (provide ceremonial cleansing) [9:13]. It was impossible for animals, ignorant of the human moral dilemma and with no control over their own destiny, to remove the sins of mankind by their shed blood. But God established the elaborate sacrificial system for a number of reasons. First, by offering a blood sacrifice, the Israelites acknowledged that atonement had to be made before God for sins. Second, they were admitting that another must make substitutionary atonement for them; thus, they could not atone for their own sins. Third, the blood atonement they offered did cover their sins before God, making it possible for Him to withhold judgment. Fourth, their sacrifices pointed to the day when Christ would once and for all atone for sin.

The Son's Obedience

Animal sacrifices were imperfect and ineffective in their ability to remove sin. In bold contrast, the writer to the Hebrews set forth the new way in which God would provide true redemption for mankind. The Son would come into the world and mediate a new covenant through the sacrifice of Himself. Not only was the Son involved, but the Father and the Holy Spirit played major roles.

The Father's Will

In quoting Psalm 40:6–8, the writer presented both the will of the Father and the will of the Son. First, it was never the will of the Father that animal sacrifices should remove sin. Three verses make this clear: "Sacrifice and offering thou wouldest not" (v. 5); "In burnt offerings and sacrifices for sin thou hast had no pleasure" (v. 6; cp. v. 8). God's displeasure must be understood in a relative sense rather than an absolute sense. God had commanded Israel to offer sacrifices, and they were to be offered from the heart (1 Sam. 15:22; Ps. 51:16; Isa. 1:11–14). God was pleased that Israel offered the sacrifices in obedience to His will, but He derived no ultimate pleasure from them because they were unable to remove sin. In contrast, the Son, in dialogue with the Father, stated the means by which He would offer sacrifice for sin: "a body hast thou prepared me" (v. 5). The Son became incarnate through the virgin birth with the express purpose of providing redemption for mankind.

Second, it was always the Father's will that the Son become the true sacrifice for sin. The Son Himself said, "Lo, I come (in the volume of the book it is written of me)" (v. 7; cp. Ps. 40:7). The Old Testament Scriptures are full of messianic prophecies concerning His first advent. After His resurrection, Christ said, "These are the words which I spoke unto you, while I was yet with you, that all things must be fulfilled, which were written in the law of Moses, and in the prophets, and in the psalms, concerning me" (Lk. 24:44; see Lk. 24:27; Jn. 5:39). The Father had foreordained "from the foundation of the world" (Rev. 13:8) that the Son would come into the world and provide for the removal of sin through His death.

Third, Christ was willing to do all of the Father's will: "Lo, I come to do thy will, 0 God" (v. 9; cp. v. 7; Ps. 40:8). With full involvement rather than passive endurance, He actively entered into the work set before Him. He was willing to come as a lowly babe in Bethlehem, live perfectly under the law, and suffer the humiliation of a criminal's death on the cross. Christ's own words sum up His commitment: "as the Father gave me commandment, even so I do" (Jn. 14:31). The conclusion is self-evident: "He taketh away the first [animal sacrifices], that he may establish the second [Christ's sacrifice]" (v. 9). Christ's sacrifice was complete in every aspect for the removal of sin, bringing about the demise of the Levitical system.

Christ, in obedience to the will of God, offered His body as a once-for-all sacrifice, making it possible for God to sanctify mankind (v. 10). Although the provision for sanctification was made by Christ, it does not become efficacious until people put their saving faith in Him. *Sanctification* means *set apart for God.* The concept is not speaking of progressive sanctification, which takes place as believers mature, but their position in Christ at the moment of salvation. The phrase "we are sanctified" (lit., having been sanctified) [v. 10] speaks of a permanent, continuous state that believers will enjoy forever.

The Son's Work

The Father's will for the removal of sin must be implemented through the work of a priesthood. The first covenant priests continually worked: "And every priest standeth daily ministering and offering often the same sacrifices" (v. 11). Hundreds of priests monotonously offered ineffectual sacrifices every day, which reminded them of sins but could "never take away sins" (remove utterly) [v. 11]. There was no seat provided for the ministering priests in either the Tabernacle or Temple, symbolizing that their work was never completed. (Sacrifices were still being offered in the Temple years after Christ's crucifixion, proving that the Epistle to the Hebrews was written before 70 A.D., when the Temple in Jerusalem was destroyed.)

Christ, who is the New Covenant priest, completed His work: "But this man, after he had offered one sacrifice for sins forever, sat down on the right hand of God" (v. 12). The contrast between the priests is significant. First, the Levitical sacrifices were continual; Christ sacrificed once for sin. Second, the Levitical priests sacrificed animals; Christ offered Himself. Third, the Levitical sacrifices only covered sin; Christ's sacrifice removed sin. Fourth, the Levitical sacrifices ceased; Christ's sacrifice is efficacious forever.

Christ is now seated "on the right hand of God" (v. 12; cp. 1:3; 8:1; 12:2), showing that He has completed His work and has been elevated to a position of power and honor. Today, Christ is ruling with the Father in heaven: "For he must reign, till he hath put all enemies under his feet" (1 Cor. 15:25; see Ps. 110:1). The enemies are the Devil with "the power of death" (2:14), the Antichrist and the false prophet (Rev. 19:20), and everyone through the centuries who has rejected Christ (Rev. 20:11–15). The expression "till his enemies be made his footstool" (v. 13) pictures a king standing with one foot on the neck of a van-quished foe. Centuries ago, conquering kings placed their feet on the necks of their defeated enemies to show total victory over them and their kingdoms. Joshua had his captains do this to the five kings he defeated (Josh. 10:23–24).

Christ is a greater Joshua; He will triumph over the powers of darkness and deliver the Kingdom to the Father at the end of the Millennium (1 Cor. 15:24–28). Christ's sacrificial ministry is summed up in one brief statement: "For by one offering [i.e., Himself] he hath perfected [brought to completion] forever them that are sanctified" (v. 14). The completeness of His expiatory ministry punctuates the Book of Hebrews (2:10; 5:9; 7:19, 28; 10:14; 11:40; 12:23) and stands forever.

The Spirit's Witness

The Holy Spirit witnesses to the completed work of Christ through the Scriptures. The witness is not *within* believers but *to* them (v. 15), as the Spirit confirms the scriptural truth already stated in the New Covenant (8:8–12). Two main concepts from the New Covenant are reviewed to show the meaning of sanctifica-tion. First, at the time of regeneration, God writes His law in the hearts and minds of believers (v. 16) by the Holy Spirit, giving them the capacity to know righteousness and live in holiness. Second, believers are justified: "their sins and iniquities will I remember no more" (v. 17). The believers' position is based on the efficacious sacrifice of Christ.

In one short verse, the irrefutable conclusion is presented: "Now where remission of these is, there is no more offering for sin" (v. 18). Because Christ's one sacrifice took away God's remem-brance of sins for those who have been redeemed, there is no longer a need to repeat the offerings. Thus, to offer sacrifices for sin is unscriptural and shows a lack of faith in Christ's finished work.

The Saints' Opportunity

Through His death, Jesus inaugurated (opened for the first time) a new (newly slain) and living (life-giving) way for people to come with boldness (confidence) into God's presence (vv. 19–20).

Because believers have this privilege, they are exhorted to exercise a fourfold commitment to the Lord.

First, believers are to be cleansed for worship. They are to "draw near with a true heart [pure and true motives] in full assurance of faith" (v. 22), anticipating the opportunity to appropriate all that God has promised to those who come before Him in a right relationship. They must approach Him having their hearts "sprinkled from an evil conscience, " which gives them bold confidence in worship.

Second, they are to have a confession before the world. They are not to waver in their faith (hope) under the fire of persecution (v. 23). Believers can take great comfort and encouragement in God's precious promise not to abandon them under any circumstance (13:5). This promise gives them strength to stand with a consistent life before a world that opposes their faith.

Third, they are to exhort others to live a life of commitment in the ministry. They are to continuously care for the welfare of their fellow Christians to provoke them to a life of "love and to good works" (v. 24) in their walk before the world and fellow believers. In love, believers are to stir each other up as they exercise the spiritual gifts that God has given them through the Holy Spirit.

Fourth, believers are exhorted not to forsake corporate worship. They are not to abandon the local church in the latter days. On the contrary, believers are to exhort one another to continue attending, especially when they know that the Lord's coming is near (v. 25).

The Sinners' Options

Christ, the once-for-all superior sacrifice, is the only sacrifice left for sin. Those rejecting Christ's sacrifice have three charges leveled against them: (1) They despise Christ by trampling Him under their feet; (2) they disregard the blood of Christ as worthless and unholy (a common thing); and (3) they do despite (insult) to the Holy Spirit who tried to draw them to Christ (v. 29).

For such rejection, the verdict is given and judgment proclaimed: "Vengeance belongeth unto me, I will recompense, saith the Lord" (v. 30). Those rejecting Christ's atoning sacrifice are considered adversaries. His adversaries under the Mosaic Covenant suffered "judgment and fiery indignation" and "died without mercy" (vv. 27–28; cp. Dt. 17:6; 32:35–36). Those rejecting Christ await the fearful judgment of God. Knowing that "It is a fearful thing to fall into the hands of the living God" (v. 31), let us examine our own commitment and then sound the warning to those who are not redeemed.

In 1873, Philip P. Bliss caught a vision of the believers' exalted position through Christ's once-for-all sacrifice on their behalf. He wrote:

Free from the law, O happy condition,
    Jesus hath bled, and there is remission;
Cursed by the law and bruised by the fall,
    Grace hath redeemed us once for all.

Now are we free—there's no condemnation,
    Jesus provides a perfect salvation;
"Come unto Me," O hear His sweet call,
    Come, and He saves us once for all.

"Children of God," O glorious calling,
    Surely His grace will keep us from falling;
Passing from death to life at His call,
    Blessed salvation once for all.

Once for all, O sinner, receive it;
    Once for all, O brother, believe it;
Cling to the cross, the burden will fall,
    Christ hath redeemed us once for all.

These words spoke Jesus, and lifted up his eyes to heaven, and said, Father, the hour is come; glorify thy Son, that thy Son also may glorify thee . . . Neither pray I for these alone, but for them also who shall believe on me through their word; That they all may be one, as thou, Father, art in me, and I in thee, that they also may be one in us; that the world may believe that thou hast sent me.

John 17:1, 20–21

CHAPTER 25

Christ, The Supplicating Priest
(John 17)

The Passover was concluded with the chanting of the Hallel Psalms. Slowly the small group made their way down the narrow stairs from the upper room, through the winding streets of Jerusalem, and across the Kidron Valley to the Garden of Gethsemane. Somewhere between the upper room and Gethsemane, possibly near the East Gate, Jesus paused to pray. Lifting His eyes heavenward, Jesus began His high priestly prayer for Himself, the disciples, and the church yet unformed.

Before us is the priestly intercession of the eternal Son of God, in the form of a servant, passionately petitioning the Father just prior to His betrayal. Most likely the disciples stood motionless, attuned to every word the Lord uttered in the Father's presence, yet understanding little of its prophetic significance. The privilege is ours to draw near and listen to the Lord's supplicating ministry as He began, "Father, the hour is come" (v. 1).

Christ Prayed for Himself

The Son's Glory

The hour had come for Jesus' departure, thus He prayed, "glorify thy Son, that thy Son also may glorify thee" (v. 1). He said "*thy* Son" not "*the* Son," taking no glory for His ministry but giving it to the Father.

Jesus manifested God's glory through His earthly ministry (v. 4), in His person (Jn. 1:14; Heb. 1:3), through miracles (Mt. 9:8), and through "power over all flesh" (v. 2). He also manifested God's glory through His finished work on the cross (v. 4; Jn. 19:30) and through His resurrection. He prayed to be returned to the heavenly relationship He enjoyed with the Father before His incarnation: "And now, O Father, glorify thou me with thine own self with the glory which I had with thee before the world was" (v. 5). When Christ took on flesh, His preincarnate glory was veiled (Phil. 2:5–8), but it was restored after His resurrection. Jesus further manifested the Father's glory by giving eternal life (v. 2) to all whom the Father had given to Him. Believers are a gift to Christ from the Father; six times in this prayer Jesus mentioned those believers given to Him by the Father (vv. 2, 6, 9, 11–12, 24).

Jesus described what is involved in receiving eternal life. Salvation comes through knowledge of "the only true God, and Jesus Christ" (v. 3), as opposed to the pagan polytheism of the world—knowledge and reception of Jesus Christ, whom "the only true God. . . hast sent" (v. 3). The conjunction *and* connects the Father and the Son; the Father cannot be known apart from the Son (Jn. 14:7–12). This is the only instance in Scriptures where Jesus called Himself "Jesus Christ" (v. 3), a strong affirmation that He is the true Messiah.

There is a threefold significance to the word *sent* (v. 3). First, it points to His deity; Jesus is the second person of the triune God who came from the Father (v. 8; Jn. 16:28). Second, it points to His incarnation (Gal. 4:4). Third, it points to His mediatorship; He is "the Apostle and High Priest of our profession [confession]" (Heb. 3:1). The word *apostle* means *one who is sent*. Christ is the high priest whom the Father sent to provide eternal life for all who will believe.

The Shared Glory

Jesus shared His glory with believers: "And the glory which thou gavest me I have given them" (v. 22). This is not the eternal glory that He possessed before His incarnation, wherein He was coequal with the Father. Rather, this is the divine glory manifested through His human nature during His earthly ministry. Believers receive this glory at the time of regeneration through the indwelling power of the Holy Spirit. Knowing the commitment of His disciples, Jesus proclaimed, "I am [have been] glorified in them" (v. 10). By receiving Jesus, the disciples were glorified in Him, and He would be glorified as they bore His name to the world. Ultimate glorification will come when believers receive their glorified bodies from the Lord (Rom. 8:30).

Jesus prayed that believers would be able to behold His glory (v. 24). The word *behold* literally means *gaze upon as a spectator.* Someday believers will gaze on the shining glory of Christ when they stand before Him.

Christ Prayed for His Followers

The Lord turned from Himself to intercede on behalf of His disciples. In the verses that follow, Jesus revealed His inner thoughts and intense love for His own as He was about to be separated from them.

The People

It should be noted that Jesus did not pray for all men: "I pray not for the world" (v. 9). Unbelievers have no access to the promises of God or the intercessory high priestly ministry of Christ. He said He interceded only for "the men whom thou gavest me out of the world" (v. 6). His intercessory ministry also reached into the future to include all believers who would, directly or indirectly, come to the Lord because of the disciples' ministry (v. 20). Believers should take great comfort in knowing that Christ interceded for them on the night of His betrayal.

Jesus said concerning those for whom He prayed, "thine they were, and thou gavest them to me" (v. 6). True, all people belong to the Father by creation, but believers belong to Him by divine election (Eph. 1:4). The elect have been given to the Son through salvation (Jn. 6:37, 39) and are kept and cared for by Him eternally (Jn. 10:27–28).

Jesus did two things for the disciples. First, He manifested the Father's name to them (v. 6)—He unveiled God's character and perfection through His perfect life and sublime teaching (Jn. 14:9–10). Second, He gave them the words (v. 8) that the Father had given to Him—the divine message of salvation and holy living. The disciples received, believed, and kept (vv. 8, 6) the name and word that the Lord imparted to them.

The Petitions

With His earthly ministry drawing to a close, Jesus said, "And now I am no more [longer] in the world" (v. 11). Soon He would leave the disciples and return to heaven, but they would remain in the world, cut off from His physical care and counsel.

He prayed "Holy Father, keep [put a guard around] through thine own name those whom thou hast given me" (v. 11). He handed His disciples back to the Father for safekeeping so "that they may be one, as we are" (v. 11). This is not speaking of an organizational, ecclesiastical, or denominational unity, but a spiritual unity in the body of Christ, which is modeled after that within the Godhead. Naturally, the disciples were not one in the same sense as the triune God. But since they were partakers of the divine nature (2 Pet. 1:4) and baptized into one body by the Holy Spirit (1 Cor. 12:13), spiritual oneness was possible.

While Jesus ministered in the world, He kept all the disciples in the Father's name but Judas, who was called "the son of perdition" (v. 12). Some people point to this verse as proof that it is possible to lose one's salvation, using Judas as an example. But the text does not say Jesus kept all *except* Judas. It says all *but* Judas, showing that Judas was never a true believer, as predicted centuries before (v. 12; cp. Ps. 41:9). Jesus mentioned "the son of perdition" in His prayer for a number of reasons. He showed that true believers are kept by God; He knew Judas would betray Him; and He knew that this betrayal was a fulfillment of prophecy.

Knowing the discouragement His disciples would feel after the crucifixion, Jesus also prayed "that they might have my joy fulfilled in themselves" (v. 13). Although He was about to be crucified, Jesus was full of the joy that came from His perfect fellowship with the Father and complete obedience to His will. The joy Jesus provides for Christians is sufficient to strengthen them, no matter how severe the world's persecution. But that joy can only be obtained by abiding in Him and drawing spiritual sustenance from Him, as a branch draws from the vine (Jn. 15:1–11). This type of joy no man can take away (Jn. 16:22).

The third petition Jesus offered for His disciples was twofold. He prayed that the Father would not "take them out of the world" (v. 15). He knew that the world would hate them because they were not of the world (v. 14). But it was necessary for them to remain in the world as witnesses, establishing and expanding His ministry. Next, He prayed that the Father "shouldest keep them from the evil [the evil one]" (v. 15). Knowing the weakness of the disciples' old nature and the power of the Devil to entrap them in sin, Jesus asked the Father to keep them from the Devil's power.

A number of comparisons can be made between the world and the disciples that apply to believers today. The world is hostile to true followers of Christ; if it hates the Master, it will hate the disciples. The disciples are controlled by Christ, the world by Satan. Although the disciples are in the world, they are alien to all it stands for.

Jesus further prayed to the Father, "Sanctify them through thy truth" (v. 17). The word *sanctified* means to be *set apart*. There are three basic concepts associated with sanctification: positional sanctification, which takes place at the moment of salvation when believers are set apart for God's use; progressive sanctification, which continually occurs as believers walk in obedience to the Word of God; and perfect sanctification, which will take place at the believers' glorification, when the old nature is eradicated and they experience completeness in body, soul, and spirit. In this instance, the Lord prayed that the disciples would be sanctified in their walk before the world.

They are sanctified by means of the truth, which is the Word of God. Jesus did not say God's Word is *true* but *truth*. Through appropriating God's Word, believers' lives are being changed into the likeness of Christ (2 Cor. 3:18).

For the disciples' sake, Jesus said, "I sanctify myself" (v. 19). Because He could not become any holier, for He was always perfect, Jesus was speaking of self-consecration. He had set Himself apart from the world's temptations and sin's defilement in order to do the Father's will. The culmination of His dedication came at the cross. Through His own sanctification, He provided sanctification for His disciples and all who would believe in the future (Heb. 10:10, 14). The words "might be sanctified" (v. 19) literally mean *have been sanctified*, showing that His disciples were already set apart for service and should live accordingly.

Jesus called the disciples to the same commission that He manifested before the world: "As thou hast sent me into the world, even so have I also sent them into the world" (v. 18); the disciples were to be Jesus' representatives in the world as He had been the Father's representative. In another place Jesus said, "the works that I do shall he do also; and greater works than these shall he do, because I go unto my Father" (Jn. 14:12). The disciples' work would be greater in extent, but not quality. Jesus, having returned to heaven, would expand His ministry through the church that was scattered throughout the world. The same commission is given in John 20:21, where Jesus mentioned the provisions of peace and power bestowed on the disciples for their mission.

Christ Prayed for His Future Followers
Prayer for Unity in the Church

As a parent prepares for the birth of a child, Jesus prevailed in supplicating prayer for future believers who would be won through the disciples' witness (v. 20). He prayed, "That they all may be one, as thou, Father, art in me, and I in thee" (v. 21). Again, this was not ecclesiastical or denominational oneness but spiritual oneness.

He went a step further and prayed, "that they also may be one in us" (v. 21). Not only is there spiritual oneness between believers, but they participate in spiritual oneness with the Godhead. The same type of unity that the Godhead manifests is to be manifested in the church. The goal for this oneness is that believers "may be made perfect in one" (v. 23). The word *perfect* means *complete* or *bring to a goal*. The ultimate realization of this oneness will take place when Christ comes for His church.

Purpose for Unity in the Church

The purpose of spiritual unity is threefold. The first purpose is "that the world may believe that thou hast sent me [Jesus]" (v. 21). Spiritual unity in the church testifies to a lost world that Christ was sent to provide salvation to all who would believe. Jesus did not say that the world would believe in Him but that they would "believe that thou [the Father] hast sent me" (v. 21). The more spiritual unity manifested by the church, the greater the impact Christ's saving power will have on the unbelieving world. The reverse is true as well. The more schism and strife, the less impact the church will have in the world.

Another purpose is "that the world may know" (v. 23) that the Father sent Jesus as Savior. When Christ sets up the Kingdom on earth, the church will have perfect unity and will clearly know that the Father sent Him.

The third purpose is "that the world may know that thou hast. . . loved them, as thou hast loved me" (v. 23). The key to spiritual unity is love within the church. Jesus said, "By this shall all men know that ye are my disciples, if ye have love one to another (Jn. 13:35; cp. 1 Jn. 3:11). When the world sees love flowing from the church, it sees the kind of love the Father has for Christ. It is a great comfort for believers to know that in a hostile world, the Father loves them as He does the Son.

Personal Unity With the Church

Jesus prayed, "Father, I will that they also . . . be with me where I am, that they may behold my glory" (v. 24). This is the first time in the prayer that Jesus said "I will," and it is in reference to the church spending eternity with Him (Jn. 14:1–3) to enjoy an incorruptible inheritance reserved in heaven for them (1 Pet. 1:4).

Jesus closed His prayer with the assurance that God's righteousness will prevail over the believers and the world. He never interceded for the world, for it does not know God (v. 25). The world is guilty of rejecting God's revelation to them, but believers know Jesus—why He came and what He has done on their behalf.

Jesus reiterated what He had done and will do for believers: "And I have declared unto them thy name, and will declare it" (v. 26; cp. v. 6). Christ is now, through the Word of God and the ministry of the Holy Spirit, revealing the Father to believers, a ministry that will continue into eternity. He is doing this so "that the love with which thou hast loved me may be in them" (v. 26). The last words of His prayer did not deal with eternal life, faith, or glory, but with love. The same love that the Father has for Jesus will fill the lives of believers. The upper room discourse began with love (Jn. 13:1) and ended with love (v. 26).

It was the Father's love that sent Jesus into a sin-cursed world to provide salvation. It was love that moved Jesus to endure the cross and become the believers' high priest. It is love for Christ that moves the church to spiritual oneness. Has love so gripped you, as a believer-priest, to intercede for those the Lord has laid on your heart? We all should say, "Father, the hour has come. I mean business with you!"

I beseech you therefore, brethren, by the mercies of God, that ye present your bodies a living sacrifice, holy, acceptable unto God, which is your reasonable service. And be not conformed to this world, but be ye transformed by the renewing of your mind, that ye may prove what is that good, and acceptable, and perfect, will of God

Romans 12:1–2

CHAPTER 26

Consecrated to Christ for Service
(Romans 12:1–2)

O n a Jerusalem hillside, a huge crowd had gathered to witness an event that would change the destiny of mankind. Darkness had filled the whole earth at noon, and it was drawing near 3 P.M. The Temple was filled with priests preparing for the evening sacrifice. A voice cried from the hillside, "Father, into thy hands I commend my spirit" (Lk. 23:46). At that moment, the Temple priests were awestruck as they heard and viewed the divine stroke of God tear in half the huge veil that hung in front of the holy of holies.

The empty room stood naked, open to all, bidding the priests to enter—a privilege no priest, except the high priest, had enjoyed since the inception of the Tabernacle. No longer was a high priest needed to annually atone for sin. Jesus, the true high priest, had opened the way for mankind to come before a holy God through His atoning blood.

Although the sacrificial system of the Old Testament ceased long ago, believers are still required to offer one more sacrifice. They are to present their bodies as a living sacrifice to the Lord.

Complete Consecration

Paul admonished Christians to "present your bodies a living sacrifice" (v. 1). The word for *present* is the same word translated *yield* in Romans 6:13 and is a voluntary, once-and-for-all act whereby believers yield their attitudes, actions, and possessions of body, soul, and spirit for God's use.

The word *present is* a technical term for offering a Levitical sacrifice. But the sacrifice of Christians is quite different from those of the Israelites, who offered substitutionary lambs, whereas Christians offer themselves. The Israelites' lambs had to be perfect; Christians offer themselves in a depraved condition and become cleansed through Christ's blood. Israelites offered dead sacrifices on the altar; Christians offer themselves as a living sacrifice for service. Israelites brought mandatory sacrifices; Christians voluntarily offer themselves.

Rather than command, Paul beseeched believers to offer themselves because of the "mercies of God" (v. 1) bestowed on them. Paul explained these mercies in Romans 1 through 11 and indicated that they include all the blessings Christians receive through redemption, justification, and sanctification through Christ's shed blood.

When believers accept Christ, they are baptized into His body (1 Cor. 12:13). Romans 6:3–5 illustrates this transaction. First, they are baptized into Christ's death (v. 3), meaning that through their identification with His crucifixion, believers died when Christ died. Second, they are identified with Christ in His burial (v. 4). As natural burial removes people from the sphere of this world, so believers are spiritually removed from the sphere of Satan's control and sin's power. Third, believers are identified with Christ in His resurrection: "For if we have been planted together in the likeness of his death, we shall be also in the likeness of his resurrection" (v. 5). Christians are resurrected to newness of life in Christ, being separated from the old life of sin. Since believers are risen with Christ, they are commanded to live in this newness of life by seeking those things that are above where Christ is seated on the right hand of God. This resurrection power, provided by Christ through the Holy Spirit, energizes Christians to live a new life for the Lord.

Four words sum up the victorious relationship of believers with Christ. First, they are to *know*, with absolute certainty, that they have been crucified, buried, and resurrected in Christ to newness of life (Rom. 6:3, 6, 9). Second, they are to *reckon* (count as a reliable fact) that sin has no more dominion over them (Rom. 6:11). Third, they are to *yield* (body, soul, and spirit) to the control of the Holy Spirit for righteousness (Rom. 6:3, 16, 19). Fourth, they are to *obey* the doctrine (teaching) that was given to them (Rom. 6:17).

Paul succinctly stated what happens to people at the time of salvation: "I am [have been] crucified with Christ: nevertheless I live; yet not I, but Christ liveth in me; and the life which I now live in the flesh I live by the faith of the Son of God, who loved me and gave himself for me" (Gal. 2:20). Because Christians have been bought with an incalculable price, they can do no less than give themselves to God as living sacrifices (1 Cor. 6:19–20).

When Christians offer themselves to God, it is considered "holy, acceptable unto God, which is your reasonable service" (Rom. 12:1). It is "holy" because they are separated to God for righteous purposes. It is "acceptable" because God is extremely pleased with such a commitment. In fact, believers' sacrifices are a delight to God! It is their "reasonable service" (logical spiritual service to perform) because they are believer-priests. This is not simply an external, ceremonial performance of duties, like that of the Levitical priesthood, but service flowing from an inner commitment to the Lord.

Even after committing their lives to Christ, Christians can be controlled by one of three forces. They can be self-centered, living only to satisfy selfish desires; they can be satanically energized to live in sin; or they can be Spirit controlled, ordering their lives according to the will of God. People become servants of whatever they yield their allegiance to—either sin or righteousness (Rom. 6:16). But Christians have been freed from sin's control to live under the Spirit's control.

Counterfeit Consecration

When Christians present their bodies as a living sacrifice, a transformation takes place. They are commanded to "be not conformed to this world" (v. 2). The word *conform* means to *fashion or shape one thing like another.* They are not to be stamped into the mold or fashioned after the image and style of the world. One translator put it well when he said, "Don't let the world around you squeeze you into its own mold" (J. B. Phillips).

"The world" (Gr., *aion*) [v. 2] refers to the spiritual and moral characteristics of the age in which believers live. Since the fall of man, all ages have been in spiritual darkness, greatly affected by Satan who is "the prince of the power of the air," but believers have been freed from this evil system, "created in Christ Jesus unto good works" (Eph. 2:1–3, 10), and do not have to yield to it.

There is much talk today about being worldly, and we could list hundreds of things that are considered worldly, but things in themselves are not worldly. It is possible to use a car, house, television, clothes, etc. for either worldliness or godliness.

Worldliness can be an action, but it is still possible to be worldly in a given area and not commit the act. For example, people might covet their neighbor's wife, house, car, or position—although never taking it—and still be worldly by desiring to possess something that does not belong to them. Thus, worldliness begins as an attitude before the act is committed. Worldliness is any attitude or action that is patterned after this world's system.

The Apostle John explained it more fully in his first epistle: "If any man love the world, the love of the Father is not in him" (1 Jn. 2:15); that is, if people habitually love the things of the world, they cannot love God at the same time. This is being worldly-minded rather than spiritually-minded.

Love for the world is manifested in three specific areas. One area is pleasure, "the lust of the flesh" (1 Jn. 2:16), which desires to satisfy the sin nature (Gal. 5:17–21). Another area is possessions, "the lust of the eyes" (1 Jn. 2:16), a desire for things, which is covetousness. The final area is pride, "the pride of life" (1 Jn. 2:16), which manifests itself in areas such as pride of possessions, position, power, prestige, or popularity. The pride of life is the motivating factor for the lust of the flesh and eyes. God hates pride (Prov. 6:16–17).

John said, "the world passeth away" (1 Jn. 2:17). The world, with its satanic system, is only temporary and is marked out for destruction. Jesus said, "Heaven and earth shall pass away, but my words shall not pass away" (Mt. 24:35). The one who "doeth the will of God abideth forever" (1 Jn. 2:17). In order to do the will of God, believers must hold to the Word of God.

"Be not conformed" (Rom. 12:2) is a command. Paul was telling Christians to stop assuming an outward expression and fashion that are patterned after the world. Believers are pilgrims and are not to fashion their conduct after a passing world system (1 Cor. 7:31). Someone has rightly stated that the spirit wedded to the world's system will be a widow tomorrow.

The key to spiritual success is doing "the will of God" (1 Jn. 2:17). In being filled with the knowledge of God's will (Col. 1:9), which comes through His Word (Ps. 119:105), believers are able to escape the world's system and abide in spiritual fellowship with God.

Conformity to Christ

Christians are to have transformed lives. *Transform* is a Greek word *(metamorphoomai)* from which the word *metamorphosis* comes. It is the same word used for Christ's transfiguration before His disciples (Mt. 17:2). The dictionary defines *metamorphosis* as "any complete change in appearance or character." This is best illustrated by the caterpillar that changes into a beautiful butterfly.

Christians are to undergo a metamorphosis at their conversion. They become new creations (2 Cor. 5:17), experiencing a complete change that is to be expressed in their outward character and conduct. In fact, they are continually being changed into the image of Christ "from glory to glory" (2 Cor. 3:18), or, to put it another way, from one successive degree of holiness to another. The commitment of Christians is maintained by the "renewing of [the] mind" (v. 2), which comes when they saturate themselves with the Word of God and prayer, so that the Holy Spirit can conform them to the image of Christ. They are to emulate the disposition and example of Christ in their thinking. Paul put it this way: "Let this mind be in you, which was also in Christ Jesus" (Phil. 2:5). Christ's mindset was one of self-denial; He emptied Himself of His divine rights, subordinated Himself to the role of a bond servant, and submitted to the death of the cross (Phil. 2:7–8). While He was on the earth, His mind was in complete surrender to the Father's will. Christians must exhibit the same type of submission if they are to be continually renewed in their spiritual life.

The key to spiritual maturity is the mind. Solomon taught that as a person "thinketh in his heart, so is he" (Prov. 23:7). The thought life is the directive to what a person is, does, or becomes. Paul said, "be renewed in the spirit of your mind" (Eph. 4:23); that is, allow the Holy Spirit to so control your mind so that every area of your life is being continually renewed and conformed to the will of God. To do this, you must "demolish arguments and every pretension that sets itself up against the knowledge of God, and. . . take captive every thought to make it obedient to Christ" (2 Cor. 10:5, NIV).

Christians whose minds are being renewed daily prove (test out by experience) [v. 2] the will of God in three ways. First, they find the will of God to be good, morally honorable, and free from all evil. God would not ask Christians to think, say, or act in ways that do not have their best interest in mind. Joseph's being sent to Egypt for God's purpose and Israel's good aptly illustrates this point (Gen. 50:20). "And we know," said Paul, "that all things work together for good to them that love God, to them who are the called according to his purpose" (Rom. 8:28).

Second, they find the will of God to be acceptable (v. 2) or well-pleasing. It may not seem well-pleasing at the outset, but believers find it to be so as they learn what God is working out in their lives. Abraham, in offering Isaac as a living sacrifice (Gen. 22), must have found it hard to understand and accept the act as God's will. But by trusting God, he passed the test and proved that the will of God is acceptable. At times, all believers find God's will difficult to understand, rather unreasonable in its demands, and, in some cases, uncceptable. But if they patiently trust God and seek His guidance, the will of God proves to be well-pleasing and the only way to live.

Third, they find the will of God to be perfect (brought to completeness) [v. 2]. The will of God is always complete for believers; nothing must be added to it.

Christians who surrender their bodies as a living sacrifice and are daily renewed by the indwelling Holy Spirit will know that the will of God is good, well-pleasing, and complete.

Although Christians have yielded their lives once for all as a living sacrifice, struggles will come to test their commitment. There will be times when they will want to crawl off the altar, take charge of their own lives, and control their own destiny. We must remember the simple but deeply profound words of Christ: "I am the vine, ye are the branches. . . without me ye can do nothing" (Jn. 15:5).

BIBLIOGRAPHY

DeHaan, M. R., *The Tabernacle* (Grand Rapids: Zondervan Publishing House, 1955).

Edersheim, A. E., *The Temple: Its Ministry and Service at the Time of Jesus Christ* (Boston: Ira Bradley & Co., 1881).

Epp, Theodore H., *Portraits of Christ in the Tabernacle* (Lincoln: Back to the Bible, 1976).

Epp, Theodore H., *Portraits of Christ in the Tabernacle*, Correspondence Course (Lincoln: Back to the Bible, 1978, Vol. I and II).

Habershon, Ada E., *Outline Studies of the Tabernacle* (London: Marshall, Morgan & Scott).

Halderman, I. M., *The Tabernacle Priesthood and Offerings* (Old Tappen: Fleming H. Revel Co., 1925).

Hottel, W. S., *Typical Truth in the Tabernacle* (Cleveland: Union Gospel Press).

Kiene, Paul F., *The Tabernacle of God in the Wilderness of Sinai* (Grand Rapids: Zondervan Publishing House, 1976).

Lockyer, Herbert, *All the Messianic Prophecies of the Bible* (Grand Rapids: Zondervan Publishing House).

Olford, Stephen F., *The Tabernacle: Camping with God* (Neptune: Loizeaux Brothers, 1973).

Patton, Edward W., *The Way Into the Holiest* (Nashville: Thomas Nelson Publishers, 1983).

Pink, Arthur W., *Gleanings in Exodus* (Chicago: Moody Press, 1973).

Slemming, C. W., *Made According to Pattern* (Fort Washington: Christian Literature Crusade, 1974).

Slemming, C. W., *These are the Garments* (Fort Washington: Christian Literature Crusade, 1974).

Slemming, C. W., *Thus Shalt Thou Serve* (Fort Washington: Christian Literature Crusade, 1974).

Soltau, Henry W., *The Tabernacle, The Priesthood, and The Offerings* (Grand Rapids: Kregel Publications, 1972).

Wemp, Sumner C., *Teaching From the Tabernacle* (Chicago: Moody Press, 1976).

More Books by
DAVID M. LEVY

JOEL: THE DAY OF THE LORD

This clear and concise commentary explains prophecies concerning the destiny of nations as they relate to Israel in the Day of the Lord. Illustrated chapter outlines and graphic representations of the prophetic events give added insight into this timely and dynamic book, which surely is one of the most neglected and misinterpreted in the bible.
ISBN-0-915540-37-1, Catalog #B32

GUARDING THE GOSPEL OF GRACE

We often lack peace, joy, or victory in our walk with Christ because we're not clear how God's grace works in our lives. The books of Galatians and Jude are brought together in this marvelous work that explains grace and what can happen if you stray from it.
ISBN 0-915540-26-6, Catalog #B67

WHEN PROPHETS SPEAK OF JUDGMENT

How close are we to the final hour? Is our nation standing on the brink of judgment? In this fascinating overview of Habakkuk, Zephaniah, and Haggai, you'll discover that the very conditions that led to Judah's downfall are all present in America today. This volume explores these conditions and issues a challenge to "redeem the time" as we move ever closer to the last days.
ISBN 0-915540-35-5, Catalog #B70

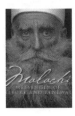

MALACHI:
MESSENGER OF REBUKE AND RENEWAL

A timeless treasure trove of practical truth, this enlightening book speaks to the human condition today. Whatever the need—social, political, or religious—you'll find the answer in this verse-by-verse, nontechnical exposition that deals with contemporary issues while providing a comprehensive chronology of Israel's prophetic history. ISBN 0-915540-20-7, Catalog #B45

REVELATION: HEARING THE LAST WORD

Why is there so much uncertainty and disagreement about the last days? What can we know about the Antichrist? In what order will the events of the last days take place? What will happen to Israel during the Tribulation? What will life be like during the Millennial Kingdom? This valuable resource will help you know what we can expect as we approach Earth's final hour. ISBN 0-915540-60-6, Catalog #B75

To order by credit card or obtain a complete catalog of all the resources available from The Friends of Israel, call us at **800-345-8461**; visit our Web store at **www.foi.org**; or write us at **P.O. Box 908, Bellmawr, NJ 08099.**